Japanese Literature: A Very Short Introduction

VERY SHORT INTRODUCTIONS are for anyone wanting a stimulating and accessible way into a new subject. They are written by experts, and have been translated into more than 45 different languages.

The series began in 1995, and now covers a wide variety of topics in every discipline. The VSI library currently contains over 700 volumes—a Very Short Introduction to everything from Psychology and Philosophy of Science to American History and Relativity—and continues to grow in every subject area.

## Very Short Introductions available now:

ABOLITIONISM Richard S. Newman
THE ABRAHAMIC RELIGIONS Charles L. Cohen
ACCOUNTING Christopher Nobes
ADDICTION Keith Humphreys
ADOLESCENCE Peter K. Smith
THEODOR W. ADORNO Andrew Bowie
ADVERTISING Winston Fletcher
AERIAL WARFARE Frank Ledwidge
AESTHETICS Bence Nanay
AFRICAN AMERICAN HISTORY Jonathan Scott Holloway
AFRICAN AMERICAN RELIGION Eddie S. Glaude Jr
AFRICAN HISTORY John Parker and Richard Rathbone
AFRICAN POLITICS Ian Taylor
AFRICAN RELIGIONS Jacob K. Olupona
AGEING Nancy A. Pachana
AGNOSTICISM Robin Le Poidevin
AGRICULTURE Paul Brassley and Richard Soffe
ALEXANDER THE GREAT Hugh Bowden
ALGEBRA Peter M. Higgins
AMERICAN BUSINESS HISTORY Walter A. Friedman
AMERICAN CULTURAL HISTORY Eric Avila
AMERICAN FOREIGN RELATIONS Andrew Preston
AMERICAN HISTORY Paul S. Boyer
AMERICAN IMMIGRATION David A. Gerber
AMERICAN INTELLECTUAL HISTORY Jennifer Ratner-Rosenhagen
THE AMERICAN JUDICIAL SYSTEM Charles L. Zelden
AMERICAN LEGAL HISTORY G. Edward White
AMERICAN MILITARY HISTORY Joseph T. Glatthaar
AMERICAN NAVAL HISTORY Craig L. Symonds
AMERICAN POETRY David Caplan
AMERICAN POLITICAL HISTORY Donald Critchlow
AMERICAN POLITICAL PARTIES AND ELECTIONS L. Sandy Maisel
AMERICAN POLITICS Richard M. Valelly
THE AMERICAN PRESIDENCY Charles O. Jones
THE AMERICAN REVOLUTION Robert J. Allison
AMERICAN SLAVERY Heather Andrea Williams
THE AMERICAN SOUTH Charles Reagan Wilson
THE AMERICAN WEST Stephen Aron
AMERICAN WOMEN'S HISTORY Susan Ware
AMPHIBIANS T. S. Kemp
ANAESTHESIA Aidan O'Donnell
ANALYTIC PHILOSOPHY Michael Beaney

ANARCHISM Alex Prichard
ANCIENT ASSYRIA Karen Radner
ANCIENT EGYPT Ian Shaw
ANCIENT EGYPTIAN ART AND ARCHITECTURE Christina Riggs
ANCIENT GREECE Paul Cartledge
ANCIENT GREEK AND ROMAN SCIENCE Liba Taub
THE ANCIENT NEAR EAST Amanda H. Podany
ANCIENT PHILOSOPHY Julia Annas
ANCIENT WARFARE Harry Sidebottom
ANGELS David Albert Jones
ANGLICANISM Mark Chapman
THE ANGLO-SAXON AGE John Blair
ANIMAL BEHAVIOUR Tristram D. Wyatt
THE ANIMAL KINGDOM Peter Holland
ANIMAL RIGHTS David DeGrazia
ANSELM Thomas Williams
THE ANTARCTIC Klaus Dodds
ANTHROPOCENE Erle C. Ellis
ANTISEMITISM Steven Beller
ANXIETY Daniel Freeman and Jason Freeman
THE APOCRYPHAL GOSPELS Paul Foster
APPLIED MATHEMATICS Alain Goriely
THOMAS AQUINAS Fergus Kerr
ARBITRATION Thomas Schultz and Thomas Grant
ARCHAEOLOGY Paul Bahn
ARCHITECTURE Andrew Ballantyne
THE ARCTIC Klaus Dodds and Jamie Woodward
HANNAH ARENDT Dana Villa
ARISTOCRACY William Doyle
ARISTOTLE Jonathan Barnes
ART HISTORY Dana Arnold
ART THEORY Cynthia Freeland
ARTIFICIAL INTELLIGENCE Margaret A. Boden
ASIAN AMERICAN HISTORY Madeline Y. Hsu
ASTROBIOLOGY David C. Catling
ASTROPHYSICS James Binney
ATHEISM Julian Baggini
THE ATMOSPHERE Paul I. Palmer
AUGUSTINE Henry Chadwick
JANE AUSTEN Tom Keymer
AUSTRALIA Kenneth Morgan
AUTISM Uta Frith
AUTOBIOGRAPHY Laura Marcus
THE AVANT GARDE David Cottington
THE AZTECS Davíd Carrasco
BABYLONIA Trevor Bryce
BACTERIA Sebastian G. B. Amyes
BANKING John Goddard and John O. S. Wilson
BARTHES Jonathan Culler
THE BEATS David Sterritt
BEAUTY Roger Scruton
LUDWIG VAN BEETHOVEN Mark Evan Bonds
BEHAVIOURAL ECONOMICS Michelle Baddeley
BESTSELLERS John Sutherland
THE BIBLE John Riches
BIBLICAL ARCHAEOLOGY Eric H. Cline
BIG DATA Dawn E. Holmes
BIOCHEMISTRY Mark Lorch
BIOGEOGRAPHY Mark V. Lomolino
BIOGRAPHY Hermione Lee
BIOMETRICS Michael Fairhurst
ELIZABETH BISHOP Jonathan F. S. Post
BLACK HOLES Katherine Blundell
BLASPHEMY Yvonne Sherwood
BLOOD Chris Cooper
THE BLUES Elijah Wald
THE BODY Chris Shilling
THE BOHEMIANS David Weir
NIELS BOHR J. L. Heilbron
THE BOOK OF COMMON PRAYER Brian Cummings
THE BOOK OF MORMON Terryl Givens
BORDERS Alexander C. Diener and Joshua Hagen
THE BRAIN Michael O'Shea
BRANDING Robert Jones
THE BRICS Andrew F. Cooper
BRITISH CINEMA Charles Barr
THE BRITISH CONSTITUTION Martin Loughlin
THE BRITISH EMPIRE Ashley Jackson
BRITISH POLITICS Tony Wright
BUDDHA Michael Carrithers

BUDDHISM Damien Keown
BUDDHIST ETHICS Damien Keown
BYZANTIUM Peter Sarris
CALVINISM Jon Balserak
ALBERT CAMUS Oliver Gloag
CANADA Donald Wright
CANCER Nicholas James
CAPITALISM James Fulcher
CATHOLICISM Gerald O'Collins
CAUSATION Stephen Mumford and Rani Lill Anjum
THE CELL Terence Allen and Graham Cowling
THE CELTS Barry Cunliffe
CHAOS Leonard Smith
GEOFFREY CHAUCER David Wallace
CHEMISTRY Peter Atkins
CHILD PSYCHOLOGY Usha Goswami
CHILDREN'S LITERATURE Kimberley Reynolds
CHINESE LITERATURE Sabina Knight
CHOICE THEORY Michael Allingham
CHRISTIAN ART Beth Williamson
CHRISTIAN ETHICS D. Stephen Long
CHRISTIANITY Linda Woodhead
CIRCADIAN RHYTHMS Russell Foster and Leon Kreitzman
CITIZENSHIP Richard Bellamy
CITY PLANNING Carl Abbott
CIVIL ENGINEERING David Muir Wood
THE CIVIL RIGHTS MOVEMENT Thomas C. Holt
CLASSICAL LITERATURE William Allan
CLASSICAL MYTHOLOGY Helen Morales
CLASSICS Mary Beard and John Henderson
CLAUSEWITZ Michael Howard
CLIMATE Mark Maslin
CLIMATE CHANGE Mark Maslin
CLINICAL PSYCHOLOGY Susan Llewelyn and Katie Aafjes-van Doorn
COGNITIVE BEHAVIOURAL THERAPY Freda McManus
COGNITIVE NEUROSCIENCE Richard Passingham
THE COLD WAR Robert J. McMahon
COLONIAL AMERICA Alan Taylor
COLONIAL LATIN AMERICAN LITERATURE Rolena Adorno
COMBINATORICS Robin Wilson
COMEDY Matthew Bevis
COMMUNISM Leslie Holmes
COMPARATIVE LITERATURE Ben Hutchinson
COMPETITION AND ANTITRUST LAW Ariel Ezrachi
COMPLEXITY John H. Holland
THE COMPUTER Darrel Ince
COMPUTER SCIENCE Subrata Dasgupta
CONCENTRATION CAMPS Dan Stone
CONDENSED MATTER PHYSICS Ross H. McKenzie
CONFUCIANISM Daniel K. Gardner
THE CONQUISTADORS Matthew Restall and Felipe Fernández-Armesto
CONSCIENCE Paul Strohm
CONSCIOUSNESS Susan Blackmore
CONTEMPORARY ART Julian Stallabrass
CONTEMPORARY FICTION Robert Eaglestone
CONTINENTAL PHILOSOPHY Simon Critchley
COPERNICUS Owen Gingerich
CORAL REEFS Charles Sheppard
CORPORATE SOCIAL RESPONSIBILITY Jeremy Moon
CORRUPTION Leslie Holmes
COSMOLOGY Peter Coles
COUNTRY MUSIC Richard Carlin
CREATIVITY Vlad Glăveanu
CRIME FICTION Richard Bradford
CRIMINAL JUSTICE Julian V. Roberts
CRIMINOLOGY Tim Newburn
CRITICAL THEORY Stephen Eric Bronner
THE CRUSADES Christopher Tyerman
CRYPTOGRAPHY Fred Piper and Sean Murphy
CRYSTALLOGRAPHY A. M. Glazer
THE CULTURAL REVOLUTION Richard Curt Kraus
DADA AND SURREALISM David Hopkins
DANTE Peter Hainsworth and David Robey
DARWIN Jonathan Howard
THE DEAD SEA SCROLLS Timothy H. Lim

DECADENCE David Weir
DECOLONIZATION Dane Kennedy
DEMENTIA Kathleen Taylor
DEMOCRACY Bernard Crick
DEMOGRAPHY Sarah Harper
DEPRESSION Jan Scott and Mary Jane Tacchi
DERRIDA Simon Glendinning
DESCARTES Tom Sorell
DESERTS Nick Middleton
DESIGN John Heskett
DEVELOPMENT Ian Goldin
DEVELOPMENTAL BIOLOGY Lewis Wolpert
THE DEVIL Darren Oldridge
DIASPORA Kevin Kenny
CHARLES DICKENS Jenny Hartley
DICTIONARIES Lynda Mugglestone
DINOSAURS David Norman
DIPLOMATIC HISTORY Joseph M. Siracusa
DOCUMENTARY FILM Patricia Aufderheide
DREAMING J. Allan Hobson
DRUGS Les Iversen
DRUIDS Barry Cunliffe
DYNASTY Jeroen Duindam
DYSLEXIA Margaret J. Snowling
EARLY MUSIC Thomas Forrest Kelly
THE EARTH Martin Redfern
EARTH SYSTEM SCIENCE Tim Lenton
ECOLOGY Jaboury Ghazoul
ECONOMICS Partha Dasgupta
EDUCATION Gary Thomas
EGYPTIAN MYTH Geraldine Pinch
EIGHTEENTH-CENTURY BRITAIN Paul Langford
THE ELEMENTS Philip Ball
EMOTION Dylan Evans
EMPIRE Stephen Howe
EMPLOYMENT LAW David Cabrelli
ENERGY SYSTEMS Nick Jenkins
ENGELS Terrell Carver
ENGINEERING David Blockley
THE ENGLISH LANGUAGE Simon Horobin
ENGLISH LITERATURE Jonathan Bate
THE ENLIGHTENMENT John Robertson
ENTREPRENEURSHIP Paul Westhead and Mike Wright
ENVIRONMENTAL ECONOMICS Stephen Smith
ENVIRONMENTAL ETHICS Robin Attfield
ENVIRONMENTAL LAW Elizabeth Fisher
ENVIRONMENTAL POLITICS Andrew Dobson
ENZYMES Paul Engel
EPICUREANISM Catherine Wilson
EPIDEMIOLOGY Rodolfo Saracci
ETHICS Simon Blackburn
ETHNOMUSICOLOGY Timothy Rice
THE ETRUSCANS Christopher Smith
EUGENICS Philippa Levine
THE EUROPEAN UNION Simon Usherwood and John Pinder
EUROPEAN UNION LAW Anthony Arnull
EVANGELICALISM John G. Stackhouse Jr.
EVIL Luke Russell
EVOLUTION Brian and Deborah Charlesworth
EXISTENTIALISM Thomas Flynn
EXPLORATION Stewart A. Weaver
EXTINCTION Paul B. Wignall
THE EYE Michael Land
FAIRY TALE Marina Warner
FAMILY LAW Jonathan Herring
MICHAEL FARADAY Frank A. J. L. James
FASCISM Kevin Passmore
FASHION Rebecca Arnold
FEDERALISM Mark J. Rozell and Clyde Wilcox
FEMINISM Margaret Walters
FILM Michael Wood
FILM MUSIC Kathryn Kalinak
FILM NOIR James Naremore
FIRE Andrew C. Scott
THE FIRST WORLD WAR Michael Howard
FLUID MECHANICS Eric Lauga
FOLK MUSIC Mark Slobin
FOOD John Krebs
FORENSIC PSYCHOLOGY David Canter
FORENSIC SCIENCE Jim Fraser
FORESTS Jaboury Ghazoul
FOSSILS Keith Thomson
FOUCAULT Gary Gutting

THE FOUNDING FATHERS R. B. Bernstein
FRACTALS Kenneth Falconer
FREE SPEECH Nigel Warburton
FREE WILL Thomas Pink
FREEMASONRY Andreas Önnerfors
FRENCH LITERATURE John D. Lyons
FRENCH PHILOSOPHY Stephen Gaukroger and Knox Peden
THE FRENCH REVOLUTION William Doyle
FREUD Anthony Storr
FUNDAMENTALISM Malise Ruthven
FUNGI Nicholas P. Money
THE FUTURE Jennifer M. Gidley
GALAXIES John Gribbin
GALILEO Stillman Drake
GAME THEORY Ken Binmore
GANDHI Bhikhu Parekh
GARDEN HISTORY Gordon Campbell
GENES Jonathan Slack
GENIUS Andrew Robinson
GENOMICS John Archibald
GEOGRAPHY John Matthews and David Herbert
GEOLOGY Jan Zalasiewicz
GEOMETRY Maciej Dunajski
GEOPHYSICS William Lowrie
GEOPOLITICS Klaus Dodds
GERMAN LITERATURE Nicholas Boyle
GERMAN PHILOSOPHY Andrew Bowie
THE GHETTO Bryan Cheyette
GLACIATION David J. A. Evans
GLOBAL CATASTROPHES Bill McGuire
GLOBAL ECONOMIC HISTORY Robert C. Allen
GLOBAL ISLAM Nile Green
GLOBALIZATION Manfred B. Steger
GOD John Bowker
GÖDEL'S THEOREM A. W. Moore
GOETHE Ritchie Robertson
THE GOTHIC Nick Groom
GOVERNANCE Mark Bevir
GRAVITY Timothy Clifton
THE GREAT DEPRESSION AND THE NEW DEAL Eric Rauchway
HABEAS CORPUS Amanda L. Tyler
HABERMAS James Gordon Finlayson
THE HABSBURG EMPIRE Martyn Rady
HAPPINESS Daniel M. Haybron
THE HARLEM RENAISSANCE Cheryl A. Wall
THE HEBREW BIBLE AS LITERATURE Tod Linafelt
HEGEL Peter Singer
HEIDEGGER Michael Inwood
THE HELLENISTIC AGE Peter Thonemann
HEREDITY John Waller
HERMENEUTICS Jens Zimmermann
HERODOTUS Jennifer T. Roberts
HIEROGLYPHS Penelope Wilson
HINDUISM Kim Knott
HISTORY John H. Arnold
THE HISTORY OF ASTRONOMY Michael Hoskin
THE HISTORY OF CHEMISTRY William H. Brock
THE HISTORY OF CHILDHOOD James Marten
THE HISTORY OF CINEMA Geoffrey Nowell-Smith
THE HISTORY OF COMPUTING Doron Swade
THE HISTORY OF LIFE Michael Benton
THE HISTORY OF MATHEMATICS Jacqueline Stedall
THE HISTORY OF MEDICINE William Bynum
THE HISTORY OF PHYSICS J. L. Heilbron
THE HISTORY OF POLITICAL THOUGHT Richard Whatmore
THE HISTORY OF TIME Leofranc Holford-Strevens
HIV AND AIDS Alan Whiteside
HOBBES Richard Tuck
HOLLYWOOD Peter Decherney
THE HOLY ROMAN EMPIRE Joachim Whaley
HOME Michael Allen Fox
HOMER Barbara Graziosi
HORMONES Martin Luck
HORROR Darryl Jones
HUMAN ANATOMY Leslie Klenerman
HUMAN EVOLUTION Bernard Wood
HUMAN PHYSIOLOGY Jamie A. Davies
HUMAN RESOURCE MANAGEMENT Adrian Wilkinson

HUMAN RIGHTS Andrew Clapham
HUMANISM Stephen Law
HUME James A. Harris
HUMOUR Noël Carroll
THE ICE AGE Jamie Woodward
IDENTITY Florian Coulmas
IDEOLOGY Michael Freeden
THE IMMUNE SYSTEM
Paul Klenerman
INDIAN CINEMA
Ashish Rajadhyaksha
INDIAN PHILOSOPHY Sue Hamilton
THE INDUSTRIAL REVOLUTION
Robert C. Allen
INFECTIOUS DISEASE Marta L. Wayne and Benjamin M. Bolker
INFINITY Ian Stewart
INFORMATION Luciano Floridi
INNOVATION Mark Dodgson and David Gann
INTELLECTUAL PROPERTY
Siva Vaidhyanathan
INTELLIGENCE Ian J. Deary
INTERNATIONAL LAW
Vaughan Lowe
INTERNATIONAL MIGRATION
Khalid Koser
INTERNATIONAL RELATIONS
Christian Reus-Smit
INTERNATIONAL SECURITY
Christopher S. Browning
INSECTS Simon Leather
IRAN Ali M. Ansari
ISLAM Malise Ruthven
ISLAMIC HISTORY Adam Silverstein
ISLAMIC LAW Mashood A. Baderin
ISOTOPES Rob Ellam
ITALIAN LITERATURE
Peter Hainsworth and David Robey
HENRY JAMES Susan L. Mizruchi
JAPANESE LITERATURE Alan Tansman
JESUS Richard Bauckham
JEWISH HISTORY David N. Myers
JEWISH LITERATURE Ilan Stavans
JOURNALISM Ian Hargreaves
JAMES JOYCE Colin MacCabe
JUDAISM Norman Solomon
JUNG Anthony Stevens
THE JURY Renée Lettow Lerner
KABBALAH Joseph Dan
KAFKA Ritchie Robertson
KANT Roger Scruton
KEYNES Robert Skidelsky
KIERKEGAARD Patrick Gardiner
KNOWLEDGE Jennifer Nagel
THE KORAN Michael Cook
KOREA Michael J. Seth
LAKES Warwick F. Vincent
LANDSCAPE ARCHITECTURE
Ian H. Thompson
LANDSCAPES AND GEOMORPHOLOGY
Andrew Goudie and Heather Viles
LANGUAGES Stephen R. Anderson
LATE ANTIQUITY Gillian Clark
LAW Raymond Wacks
THE LAWS OF THERMODYNAMICS
Peter Atkins
LEADERSHIP Keith Grint
LEARNING Mark Haselgrove
LEIBNIZ Maria Rosa Antognazza
C. S. LEWIS James Como
LIBERALISM Michael Freeden
LIGHT Ian Walmsley
LINCOLN Allen C. Guelzo
LINGUISTICS Peter Matthews
LITERARY THEORY Jonathan Culler
LOCKE John Dunn
LOGIC Graham Priest
LOVE Ronald de Sousa
MARTIN LUTHER Scott H. Hendrix
MACHIAVELLI Quentin Skinner
MADNESS Andrew Scull
MAGIC Owen Davies
MAGNA CARTA Nicholas Vincent
MAGNETISM Stephen Blundell
MALTHUS Donald Winch
MAMMALS T. S. Kemp
MANAGEMENT John Hendry
NELSON MANDELA Elleke Boehmer
MAO Delia Davin
MARINE BIOLOGY Philip V. Mladenov
MARKETING
Kenneth Le Meunier-FitzHugh
THE MARQUIS DE SADE John Phillips
MARTYRDOM Jolyon Mitchell
MARX Peter Singer
MATERIALS Christopher Hall
MATHEMATICAL FINANCE
Mark H. A. Davis
MATHEMATICS Timothy Gowers
MATTER Geoff Cottrell

THE MAYA Matthew Restall and Amara Solari
THE MEANING OF LIFE Terry Eagleton
MEASUREMENT David Hand
MEDICAL ETHICS Michael Dunn and Tony Hope
MEDICAL LAW Charles Foster
MEDIEVAL BRITAIN John Gillingham and Ralph A. Griffiths
MEDIEVAL LITERATURE Elaine Treharne
MEDIEVAL PHILOSOPHY John Marenbon
MEMORY Jonathan K. Foster
METAPHYSICS Stephen Mumford
METHODISM William J. Abraham
THE MEXICAN REVOLUTION Alan Knight
MICROBIOLOGY Nicholas P. Money
MICROBIOMES Angela E. Douglas
MICROECONOMICS Avinash Dixit
MICROSCOPY Terence Allen
THE MIDDLE AGES Miri Rubin
MILITARY JUSTICE Eugene R. Fidell
MILITARY STRATEGY Antulio J. Echevarria II
JOHN STUART MILL Gregory Claeys
MINERALS David Vaughan
MIRACLES Yujin Nagasawa
MODERN ARCHITECTURE Adam Sharr
MODERN ART David Cottington
MODERN BRAZIL Anthony W. Pereira
MODERN CHINA Rana Mitter
MODERN DRAMA Kirsten E. Shepherd-Barr
MODERN FRANCE Vanessa R. Schwartz
MODERN INDIA Craig Jeffrey
MODERN IRELAND Senia Pašeta
MODERN ITALY Anna Cento Bull
MODERN JAPAN Christopher Goto-Jones
MODERN LATIN AMERICAN LITERATURE Roberto González Echevarría
MODERN WAR Richard English
MODERNISM Christopher Butler
MOLECULAR BIOLOGY Aysha Divan and Janice A. Royds
MOLECULES Philip Ball
MONASTICISM Stephen J. Davis
THE MONGOLS Morris Rossabi
MONTAIGNE William M. Hamlin
MOONS David A. Rothery
MORMONISM Richard Lyman Bushman
MOUNTAINS Martin F. Price
MUHAMMAD Jonathan A. C. Brown
MULTICULTURALISM Ali Rattansi
MULTILINGUALISM John C. Maher
MUSIC Nicholas Cook
MUSIC AND TECHNOLOGY Mark Katz
MYTH Robert A. Segal
NANOTECHNOLOGY Philip Moriarty
NAPOLEON David A. Bell
THE NAPOLEONIC WARS Mike Rapport
NATIONALISM Steven Grosby
NATIVE AMERICAN LITERATURE Sean Teuton
NAVIGATION Jim Bennett
NAZI GERMANY Jane Caplan
NEGOTIATION Carrie Menkel-Meadow
NEOLIBERALISM Manfred B. Steger and Ravi K. Roy
NETWORKS Guido Caldarelli and Michele Catanzaro
THE NEW TESTAMENT Luke Timothy Johnson
THE NEW TESTAMENT AS LITERATURE Kyle Keefer
NEWTON Robert Iliffe
NIETZSCHE Michael Tanner
NINETEENTH-CENTURY BRITAIN Christopher Harvie and H. C. G. Matthew
THE NORMAN CONQUEST George Garnett
NORTH AMERICAN INDIANS Theda Perdue and Michael D. Green
NORTHERN IRELAND Marc Mulholland
NOTHING Frank Close
NUCLEAR PHYSICS Frank Close
NUCLEAR POWER Maxwell Irvine
NUCLEAR WEAPONS Joseph M. Siracusa
NUMBER THEORY Robin Wilson
NUMBERS Peter M. Higgins

NUTRITION David A. Bender
OBJECTIVITY Stephen Gaukroger
OCEANS Dorrik Stow
THE OLD TESTAMENT Michael D. Coogan
THE ORCHESTRA D. Kern Holoman
ORGANIC CHEMISTRY Graham Patrick
ORGANIZATIONS Mary Jo Hatch
ORGANIZED CRIME Georgios A. Antonopoulos and Georgios Papanicolaou
ORTHODOX CHRISTIANITY A. Edward Siecienski
OVID Llewelyn Morgan
PAGANISM Owen Davies
PAKISTAN Pippa Virdee
THE PALESTINIAN-ISRAELI CONFLICT Martin Bunton
PANDEMICS Christian W. McMillen
PARTICLE PHYSICS Frank Close
PAUL E. P. Sanders
IVAN PAVLOV Daniel P. Todes
PEACE Oliver P. Richmond
PENTECOSTALISM William K. Kay
PERCEPTION Brian Rogers
THE PERIODIC TABLE Eric R. Scerri
PHILOSOPHICAL METHOD Timothy Williamson
PHILOSOPHY Edward Craig
PHILOSOPHY IN THE ISLAMIC WORLD Peter Adamson
PHILOSOPHY OF BIOLOGY Samir Okasha
PHILOSOPHY OF LAW Raymond Wacks
PHILOSOPHY OF MIND Barbara Gail Montero
PHILOSOPHY OF PHYSICS David Wallace
PHILOSOPHY OF SCIENCE Samir Okasha
PHILOSOPHY OF RELIGION Tim Bayne
PHOTOGRAPHY Steve Edwards
PHYSICAL CHEMISTRY Peter Atkins
PHYSICS Sidney Perkowitz
PILGRIMAGE Ian Reader
PLAGUE Paul Slack
PLANETARY SYSTEMS Raymond T. Pierrehumbert
PLANETS David A. Rothery
PLANTS Timothy Walker
PLATE TECTONICS Peter Molnar
PLATO Julia Annas
POETRY Bernard O'Donoghue
POLITICAL PHILOSOPHY David Miller
POLITICS Kenneth Minogue
POLYGAMY Sarah M. S. Pearsall
POPULISM Cas Mudde and Cristóbal Rovira Kaltwasser
POSTCOLONIALISM Robert J. C. Young
POSTMODERNISM Christopher Butler
POSTSTRUCTURALISM Catherine Belsey
POVERTY Philip N. Jefferson
PREHISTORY Chris Gosden
PRESOCRATIC PHILOSOPHY Catherine Osborne
PRIVACY Raymond Wacks
PROBABILITY John Haigh
PROGRESSIVISM Walter Nugent
PROHIBITION W. J. Rorabaugh
PROJECTS Andrew Davies
PROTESTANTISM Mark A. Noll
PSEUDOSCIENCE Michael D. Gordin
PSYCHIATRY Tom Burns
PSYCHOANALYSIS Daniel Pick
PSYCHOLOGY Gillian Butler and Freda McManus
PSYCHOLOGY OF MUSIC Elizabeth Hellmuth Margulis
PSYCHOPATHY Essi Viding
PSYCHOTHERAPY Tom Burns and Eva Burns-Lundgren
PUBLIC ADMINISTRATION Stella Z. Theodoulou and Ravi K. Roy
PUBLIC HEALTH Virginia Berridge
PURITANISM Francis J. Bremer
THE QUAKERS Pink Dandelion
QUANTUM THEORY John Polkinghorne
RACISM Ali Rattansi
RADIOACTIVITY Claudio Tuniz
RASTAFARI Ennis B. Edmonds
READING Belinda Jack
THE REAGAN REVOLUTION Gil Troy
REALITY Jan Westerhoff
RECONSTRUCTION Allen C. Guelzo
THE REFORMATION Peter Marshall
REFUGEES Gil Loescher
RELATIVITY Russell Stannard
RELIGION Thomas A. Tweed

RELIGION IN AMERICA Timothy Beal
THE RENAISSANCE Jerry Brotton
RENAISSANCE ART
Geraldine A. Johnson
RENEWABLE ENERGY Nick Jelley
REPTILES T.S. Kemp
REVOLUTIONS Jack A. Goldstone
RHETORIC Richard Toye
RISK Baruch Fischhoff and John Kadvany
RITUAL Barry Stephenson
RIVERS Nick Middleton
ROBOTICS Alan Winfield
ROCKS Jan Zalasiewicz
ROMAN BRITAIN Peter Salway
THE ROMAN EMPIRE
Christopher Kelly
THE ROMAN REPUBLIC
David M. Gwynn
ROMANTICISM Michael Ferber
ROUSSEAU Robert Wokler
RUSSELL A. C. Grayling
THE RUSSIAN ECONOMY
Richard Connolly
RUSSIAN HISTORY Geoffrey Hosking
RUSSIAN LITERATURE Catriona Kelly
THE RUSSIAN REVOLUTION
S. A. Smith
SAINTS Simon Yarrow
SAMURAI Michael Wert
SAVANNAS Peter A. Furley
SCEPTICISM Duncan Pritchard
SCHIZOPHRENIA
Chris Frith and Eve Johnstone
SCHOPENHAUER
Christopher Janaway
SCIENCE AND RELIGION
Thomas Dixon and Adam R. Shapiro
SCIENCE FICTION David Seed
THE SCIENTIFIC REVOLUTION
Lawrence M. Principe
SCOTLAND Rab Houston
SECULARISM Andrew Copson
SEXUAL SELECTION Marlene Zuk and
Leigh W. Simmons
SEXUALITY Véronique Mottier
WILLIAM SHAKESPEARE
Stanley Wells
SHAKESPEARE'S COMEDIES Bart van Es
SHAKESPEARE'S SONNETS AND
POEMS Jonathan F. S. Post
SHAKESPEARE'S TRAGEDIES
Stanley Wells
GEORGE BERNARD SHAW
Christopher Wixson
MARY SHELLEY Charlotte Gordon
THE SHORT STORY Andrew Kahn
SIKHISM Eleanor Nesbitt
SILENT FILM Donna Kornhaber
THE SILK ROAD James A. Millward
SLANG Jonathon Green
SLEEP Steven W. Lockley and
Russell G. Foster
SMELL Matthew Cobb
ADAM SMITH Christopher J. Berry
SOCIAL AND CULTURAL
ANTHROPOLOGY
John Monaghan and Peter Just
SOCIAL PSYCHOLOGY Richard J. Crisp
SOCIAL WORK Sally Holland and
Jonathan Scourfield
SOCIALISM Michael Newman
SOCIOLINGUISTICS John Edwards
SOCIOLOGY Steve Bruce
SOCRATES C. C. W. Taylor
SOFT MATTER Tom McLeish
SOUND Mike Goldsmith
SOUTHEAST ASIA James R. Rush
THE SOVIET UNION Stephen Lovell
THE SPANISH CIVIL WAR
Helen Graham
SPANISH LITERATURE Jo Labanyi
THE SPARTANS Andrew J. Bayliss
SPINOZA Roger Scruton
SPIRITUALITY Philip Sheldrake
SPORT Mike Cronin
STARS Andrew King
STATISTICS David J. Hand
STEM CELLS Jonathan Slack
STOICISM Brad Inwood
STRUCTURAL ENGINEERING
David Blockley
STUART BRITAIN John Morrill
SUBURBS Carl Abbott
THE SUN Philip Judge
SUPERCONDUCTIVITY
Stephen Blundell
SUPERSTITION Stuart Vyse
SYMMETRY Ian Stewart
SYNAESTHESIA Julia Simner
SYNTHETIC BIOLOGY Jamie A. Davies

SYSTEMS BIOLOGY Eberhard O. Voit
TAXATION Stephen Smith
TEETH Peter S. Ungar
TELESCOPES Geoff Cottrell
TERRORISM Charles Townshend
THEATRE Marvin Carlson
THEOLOGY David F. Ford
THINKING AND REASONING Jonathan St B. T. Evans
THOUGHT Tim Bayne
TIBETAN BUDDHISM Matthew T. Kapstein
TIDES David George Bowers and Emyr Martyn Roberts
TIME Jenann Ismael
TOCQUEVILLE Harvey C. Mansfield
LEO TOLSTOY Liza Knapp
TOPOLOGY Richard Earl
TRAGEDY Adrian Poole
TRANSLATION Matthew Reynolds
THE TREATY OF VERSAILLES Michael S. Neiberg
TRIGONOMETRY Glen Van Brummelen
THE TROJAN WAR Eric H. Cline
TRUST Katherine Hawley
THE TUDORS John Guy
TWENTIETH-CENTURY BRITAIN Kenneth O. Morgan
TYPOGRAPHY Paul Luna
THE UNITED NATIONS Jussi M. Hanhimäki
UNIVERSITIES AND COLLEGES David Palfreyman and Paul Temple
THE U.S. CIVIL WAR Louis P. Masur
THE U.S. CONGRESS Donald A. Ritchie
THE U.S. CONSTITUTION David J. Bodenhamer
THE U.S. SUPREME COURT Linda Greenhouse
UTILITARIANISM Katarzyna de Lazari-Radek and Peter Singer
UTOPIANISM Lyman Tower Sargent
VATICAN II Shaun Blanchard and Stephen Bullivant
VETERINARY SCIENCE James Yeates
THE VIKINGS Julian D. Richards
VIOLENCE Philip Dwyer
THE VIRGIN MARY Mary Joan Winn Leith
THE VIRTUES Craig A. Boyd and Kevin Timpe
VIRUSES Dorothy H. Crawford
VOLCANOES Michael J. Branney and Jan Zalasiewicz
VOLTAIRE Nicholas Cronk
WAR AND RELIGION Jolyon Mitchell and Joshua Rey
WAR AND TECHNOLOGY Alex Roland
WATER John Finney
WAVES Mike Goldsmith
WEATHER Storm Dunlop
THE WELFARE STATE David Garland
WITCHCRAFT Malcolm Gaskill
WITTGENSTEIN A. C. Grayling
WORK Stephen Fineman
WORLD MUSIC Philip Bohlman
WORLD MYTHOLOGY David Leeming
THE WORLD TRADE ORGANIZATION Amrita Narlikar
WORLD WAR II Gerhard L. Weinberg
WRITING AND SCRIPT Andrew Robinson
ZIONISM Michael Stanislawski
ÉMILE ZOLA Brian Nelson

Available soon:

OBSERVATIONAL ASTRONOMY Geoff Cottrell
MATHEMATICAL ANALYSIS Richard Earl
HISTORY OF EMOTIONS Thomas Dixon

For more information visit our website

www.oup.com/vsi/

Alan Tansman

# JAPANESE LITERATURE

## A Very Short Introduction

OXFORD
UNIVERSITY PRESS

Oxford University Press is a department of the University of Oxford.
It furthers the University's objective of excellence in research, scholarship,
and education by publishing worldwide. Oxford is a registered trade mark of
Oxford University Press in the UK and certain other countries.

Published in the United States of America by Oxford University Press
198 Madison Avenue, New York, NY 10016, United States of America.



Library of Congress Cataloging-in-Publication Data

Names: Tansman, Alan, 1960- author.
Title: Japanese literature : a very short introduction / Alan Tansman.
Description: New York, NY : Oxford University Press, [2023] |
Includes bibliographical references and index.
Identifiers: LCCN 2022058581 (print) | LCCN 2022058582 (ebook) |
ISBN 9780199765256 (paperback) | ISBN 9780190933913 (epub)
Subjects: LCSH: Japanese literature—History and criticism. |
LCGFT: Literary criticism.
Classification: LCC PL717 .T36 2023 (print) | LCC PL717 (ebook) |
DDC 895.609—dc23/eng/20230104
LC record available at https://lccn.loc.gov/2022058581
LC ebook record available at https://lccn.loc.gov/2022058582

Printed and bound by
CPI Group (UK) Ltd, Croydon, CR0 4YY

# Contents

# List of illustrations

# Acknowledgments

In writing this book I have humbly drawn upon the work of many wonderful scholars, whose names appear in the References section. Those of them who happen to read this book will notice their own thinking and formulations guiding my own. They will also recognize my creative borrowing to be in tune with the Japanese aesthetic tradition itself. I have leaned especially on H. Mack Horton, Ian Levy, Earl Miner, Thomas Hare, Mark Morris, Donald Keene, and Esperanza Ramirez-Christensen for the classical Japanese canon; on Joel Cohn and Matthew Fargo for the comic tradition; on Reiko Auestad, Paul Roquet, Keith Vincent, and Jonathan Zwicker for modern and contemporary literature; and on Dennis Washburn for *The Tale of Genji*.

I thank the following people who read the book at various stages: Pedro Bassoe, Jennifer Crewe, H. Mack Horton, Victoria Kahn, Matthew Mewhinney, and James Reichert. For multiple very close and patient and life-saving readings I thank Greg Pflugfelder, Paula Varsano, and Alejandro Yarza.

All of these people know as keenly as I do that this book only hints at the riches of a great literary corpus.

# A note on Japanese names

Names appear in Japanese order, surname (family name) first. If an author commonly goes by a pen name, I use the pen name in subsequent references, except in the index, which is organized by surname. To give an example, I refer to Natsume Sôseki as Sôseki because that is his pen name. Ôe Kenzaburô is referred to as Ôe, his surname.

# Chapter 1
# A world of words

The concrete and the glittering—these aesthetic qualities suffuse the Japanese literary tradition. In the hands of its greatest practitioners, Japanese literature describes transparently the world available to the senses. It is also keyed to worlds evoked by other literary languages, both native and foreign, and to an atmosphere hovering beyond the reach of language.

Early on, and for many centuries, the central literary point of reference was China, and then, later, Europe and the United States. This did not reflect a lack of interest in immediate, lived experience, however, as much as it did the belief that tapping into the power of other and older literary languages would more effectively stir—at least in similarly educated readers—emotions that felt real and create reverberations that extended beyond the words. The deepest roots of this aesthetic sensibility may lie both in Japanese literature's early linguistic and philosophical Chinese influence, and in the Buddhist skepticism regarding language's capacity to capture and convey reality. The awareness that explicatory language, by its very nature, falls short of accurate representation infused the tradition virtually from the beginning and quickly became a defining quality reflected upon and reinforced by subsequent literary work.

The permeation of a Buddhist sensibility into this conception of the limitations of language—and the creative output unleashed by working against such limitations—cannot be underestimated. To live is to suffer because we become attached to things—possessions, emotions, beauty, and even our own egos. And even as we cannot trust that words do point beyond those things to some truth behind them, they remain the most unshakeable object of literary attachment. This great irony suffuses the tradition.



The momentous historical contingency of having been born from within the ancient and immense body of Chinese literary creation made the business of literature seem to its practitioners to be less about the world than about another literature, or even literature itself. Over the sixth and seventh centuries, Japanese officialdom absorbed a rich corpus of Chinese literature; by the ninth century, four Japanese anthologies of Chinese poetry would be produced and widely circulated. Although the centuries to come would see a shift in emphasis toward the development of native forms, and a sharpened consciousness of a specific Japanese literary history, Chinese literature would remain Japanese literature's inspiration until the late nineteenth century. Born self-consciously in relationship to another literature, Japanese literary writing manifested in its very bones the sense that any experienced, inspiring world out there was itself created out of words.

For classical Japanese writers, the practice of what we might call intertextuality was a way of negotiating a simultaneous sense of Japan's position at the cultural center and cultural periphery in relation to China; and later, for the moderns, in relation to Europe. In the tradition's earliest days, textual creativity was unleashed by the collision between spoken Japanese and written Chinese in the fifth and sixth centuries, giving rise to a fruitful literary hybridity. In fact, there had been no Japanese writing system before that moment when Chinese characters arrived on the scene, brought to Japan with the spread of Buddhist scriptures and the circulation of classical writings of Chinese statecraft. The particularities of the Chinese writing system brought with it, too, its own inherent literary features. Though Chinese characters can represent both a sound and a meaning in the Japanese language, they can also indicate meaning independent of Japanese pronunciation and sounds independent of meaning.

By the eighth century, there developed the practice of reading Chinese as if it were Japanese, referred to at times as *kundoku*. In this practice, Chinese characters were assigned Japanese pronunciations, and diacritical marks were added to indicate the order in which the characters should be read to accord with Japanese syntax. In other words, readers learned to look at a text as if at a palimpsest and in their minds rearrange the words. We might assume that to read *kundoku* was to be constantly reminded that languages are never simply, and purely, naturally given, and that they are never purely "native."

By the end of the ninth century, this method of reading had become a style of writing as well. Two phonetic scripts developed, allowing Japanese to be written largely phonetically, without Chinese characters. *Kundoku* was not simply a method of reading, for it permitted Japanese writers familiar with its conventions to *write* in classical Chinese too. From this there developed an array of writing styles, ranging from orthodox classical Chinese to highly modified styles adapted to the Japanese language. This writing is today referred to as *kanbun*, or Chinese writing, and *kanbun* would continue on as the elite written language used by government officials and religious institutions well into the nineteenth century. But logographic script was not the only route open to early Japanese writers, for it was understood from the outset that Chinese characters could be used phonetically to represent Japanese sounds. By the end of the ninth century, a gradual process of graphical simplification had given rise to two abbreviated phonetic scripts, allowing easier transcription of vernacular Japanese and setting the stage for an efflorescence of vernacular literature. It is no coincidence that the classics of vernacular literature were written by women, barred as they were from official capacities and less schooled in Chinese.

Early evidence of this linguistic situation is found in the courtier Ô no Yasumaro's preface to the early eighth-century *Kojiki* (*Record of Ancient Matters*)—a repository of Japanese origin myths that he compiled (and that came to be treated as a literary work only in the 1920s), which he presented at court to the sovereign. The preface explains, in Chinese, that he was requested to transcribe and edit an oral historical record, which had been recounted to him by a female reciter. Because Japanese as yet had no writing system of its own, he used Chinese characters phonetically, irrespective of their meanings, to register the pronunciations of the names of Japanese gods, people, and places. His solution, in other words, was to employ the method the Chinese had used to transliterate, rather than translate, Sanskrit terms.



This practice may have helped confirm rather than counter the sense of a disconnect between the written and the spoken word. An awareness of the near-inaccessibility of sound behind the silent art of writing is manifest in the ways in which writers would reach toward the uncanny, the fading away, the turning into nothing, the somewhere-beyond-representation. Even before the struggle to transcribe ideas in writing, there had arisen a word to capture language's capacity to articulate something without uttering it. That word is *kotodama*, and it refers to the power of language to create and transform the world. It first appears in the earliest Japanese poetic anthology, the eighth-century *Man'yôshû* (*Collection of Ten Thousand Leaves*) whose 4,500 poems record such things as divination rituals, blessings on the land, commemorations of excursions, and memorialization of the dead.

The range of content suggests that the very earliest Japanese poems, those predating the anthology, may have closely resembled Buddhist magical incantations; and, indeed, by the twelfth century the "way of the Buddha" was likened to "the way of poetry." *Kotodama*, there at the very start of the tradition, then embedded itself deeply in Japan's literary sensibility, and has survived there down to the present.

Japanese literature clings to the concrete immediacy of the phenomenal world evoking the phantom quality of phenomena, the shadow of evanescence that hangs over all things. This has been the poetic legacy of Buddhism. In this sense the literature has always been one that is both secular and enchanted. From its first great poet, the seventh- to eighth-century courtier-poet Kakinomoto no Hitomaro, to its best-selling modern-day author, Murakami Haruki, it has been attached to this world but has had hovering about it glimmers of other worlds. It has excelled at expressing the invisible in concrete terms. For millennia this enchantment was written through words referring not to things out there but to other words, not to life but to other literatures. Literary play itself was a form of enchantment. Japanese literature has been said to be about nature. But it only used words referring to nature to get at what cannot be seen. This is not to say that Japanese literature has been concerned only with formal matters. It has been an incarnational art whose concrete details make felt the mystery of being alive.



Poetry that records the personal, lyric voice has, since the eighth century, occupied a central position in Japanese literary creation. The art of narrative only emerged from the poetic substratum to blossom, in the eleventh century, into one of Japan's great literary masterpieces, *The Tale of Genji*. Over the course of the centuries Japanese literature developed other genres no less important than poetry and narrative, among them the diary, the essay, drama, the picture book, and the literary treatise.

Uniting these many genres of prose writing—including narrative—is, always, a manifest lyric impulse. Whether long or short, narrative displays a penchant more for the poetic fragment than for the great narrative arc. Even those that center on and sustain the most complex plots tend to roam and spread, stopping frequently for epiphanies along the way.

Central to the common understanding of Japanese literature is the staying power, the conservative pull, of literary forms—and the attempt to radically break with them in modernity. That break was made by the bold and creative work of writers who tried to overturn a centuries-old practice of literary invention that demanded tremendous restraint in form and diction. Some of these writers broke through the web of classical diction and form to write prosaically, realistically, of the world before them. Many of the most creative writers made the rending of that past literary veil less important than the forging of new prose styles tinctured both by past forms and by contemporary forms from outside of Japan itself.



In short, Japanese literature is a literature of resonance, in which words work less to represent things as such than they do to connote something beyond. From its beginnings in the eighth century through the last quarter of the nineteenth, when writers began to strive for transparent realism, it reached toward this "beyond" through a literature that refers first and foremost to other literature, and not to the world itself. It has been an art whose concrete details have made felt the vibrations of emotions and of the nonmaterial world. And it is not to say that Japanese literature has not addressed the world. Particularly in the modern period, it has done so with a vengeance. But even when it has, its most interesting writers have reached through this world's things to something hovering beyond and have been acutely aware of the inaccessibility of the world except as written through a screen of literary figuration.

For two of the great readers of the tradition, literature that seemed to refer to nature only referred to other literary worlds. In the eighteenth century, the philologist and close textual reader Motoori Norinaga argued that Japanese poetry (called for centuries before his time *waka*, meaning Japanese song, as opposed to Chinese poetry) enacts and performs emotion—a melancholy sensitivity for the transience of things, or *mono no aware*—through literary turnings. For him, poetry, as it was practiced in the tradition, did not *mean* anything. Earlier, in the thirteenth century, Fujiwara Teika, one of the tradition's greatest poets and most influential poetic theorists, argued that the most powerful poetry was concerned not at all with persuasively portraying its subject matter but with dipping into a trove of past literature and the masterly manipulation of formal literary devices.

That Japanese literature was nestled within a mesh of words was an aesthetic ideal that had been present as far back as the early tenth century. In his preface to the 905 *Kokinshû* (*Collection of Poems Ancient and Modern*), the inaugural anthology of a total of twenty-one imperially commissioned anthologies of Japanese poetry, its chief compiler (who was also a major poet and literary thinker), Ki no Tsurayuki, wrote:



> The seeds of Japanese poetry lie in the human heart and grow into leaves of ten thousand words. Many things happen to the people of this world, and all they think and feel is given expression in description of things they see and hear. When we hear the warbling of the mountain thrush in the blossoms or the voice of the frog in the water, we know every living being has its song. It is poetry that, without effort, moves heaven and earth, stirs the feelings of the invisible gods and spirits, smoothens the relations of men and women, and calms the hearts of fierce warriors.

Tsurayuki speaks of poetry as a natural emanation of a feeling heart—as leaves that grow. But these leaves are words. The "leaves of ten thousand words" alludes to the title of Japan's first collection of poetry, the *Man'yôshû*. The very conception and arrangement of the preface reads almost like a free translation (or a pointed emendation) of the Han Dynasty exegete, Mao Heng's "Great Preface" to the early seventh-century BCE Chinese *Book of Odes*.

For Fujiwara Shunzei, the twelfth-century poet and literary theorist, Tsurayuki's argument was less about poetry's direct response to things than it was about poetry's emergence from within a web of poetry, as he wrote in 1197: "As stated in the preface to the *Kokinshû*, the seeds of Japanese poetry lie in the human heart and grow into leaves of ten thousand words. Thus, without Japanese poetry, even if people visited the spring blossoms or viewed the autumn leaves, no one would know their color or splendor."



The *Kokinshû* provides a snapshot of Japanese court poetry as it was practiced from the early ninth to early tenth centuries, with the familiar themes of the progression of seasons, the natural world, love affairs and their demises, mourning, and travel. The poems are carefully arranged according to theme and imagery. Together, they present the aesthetic ideal of writing poems that convey mental states strictly through poetic figuration. In his preface, Tsurayuki set out to establish a canon, and he succeeded, setting forth the aesthetic terms that would guide Japanese poets for centuries to come. These included *sama*, or obliqueness and wit; *kotoba*, or elegant diction and style; and *kokoro*, or the "spirit" of the poem. Japanese poetry's task was now to find the proper balance between diction, *kotoba*, and spirit, *kokoro*. On display in the collection are poetic techniques inherited from the *Man'yôshû*, including the *makurakotoba* or "pillow word," set figures of speech "pillowing" a noun or verb. On display also are more contemporary innovations, such as the *kakekotoba* or "pivot word," a punning connection binding metaphorical links into a closer, more complex relationship, as in this anonymous poem:

if in swiftly
flowing rapids seaweed could
grow I'd sow some in
the river of tears that floods
my sleeves then I might see you

The Japanese word for "seaweed" is homophonic with the word for "chance to meet," so "if seaweed could grow" also reads as the phrase "if we have a chance to meet."

Here is another example, by the ninth-century woman poet Ono no Komachi, named by Tsurayuki as one of the "Six Immortal Poets":

colors of
blossoms faded and passed
to no purpose
days wasted in pensive gazing
the long rains fall



The word translated here as "fall" is homophonic with the word "grow old," and "long rains" sounds like "pensive gazing." The "colors of the blossoms" is a metaphor for Komachi's own erotic beauty, which has likewise faded. Then there are the *engo*, associative words: words that, over time, have come to be associated in the mind of the poet and the listener less with the world out there than to words and their poetic usage.

Tsurayuki championed a decorous balance between the words (*kotoba*) and their spirit (*kokoro*). He faults all six of the canonized "poetic immortals" for failing to achieve this balance. In fact, he created his own anthology because he felt that even the *Kokinshû*, designed by committee, did not effectively strike the balance he desired. For Tsurayuki, wordplay is sterile without a commensurate and appropriate content.

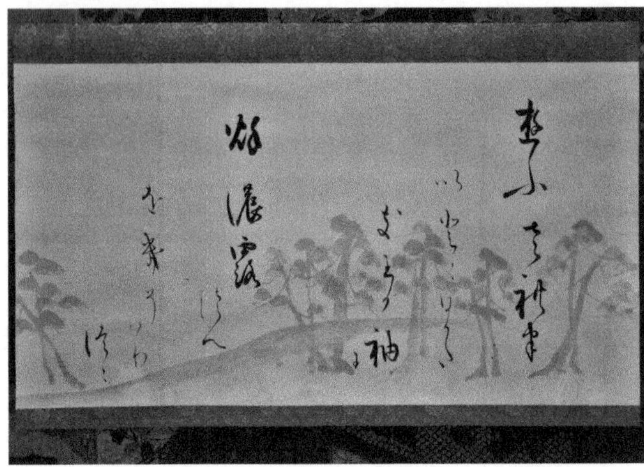

**1. This seventeenth-century calligraphic rendering of a poem from *Collection of Poems Ancient and Modern* races across golden, abstract images of pine trees, conveying the anguish of a suffering woman in a state of unrequited love, crying into her sleeve. The rushing movement of the black ink, held in check by the precision of the writing, gives expression to that complex emotional state.**

Before the *Kokinshû* set a precedent demanding strict, decorous restraint on artistic individuality and became the textual wellspring (but also straitjacket) of later poetry, there was a poet whose lyric voice so powerfully expressed the anguish of personal suffering that the architecture of poetic convention seemed to fade before the power of his personal voice.

If, as is commonly held, poetry is at the heart of Japanese literature, and if the very heart of the tradition is the *Man'yôshû*, then the poet at the very heart of this revered heart of the classical poetic tradition is the courtier Kakinomoto no Hitomaro. In the *Man'yôshû* we find long and short forms; prose narratives; visual and oral aesthetic effects; the jostling of Chinese and Japanese forms; Buddhist and Daoist sensibilities; the mark of Silk Road culture; magical poetic practice; poetry as public, political work;

longing, evanescence, and sadness; complex allusiveness and other forms of wordplay; narrative development through associative progression; objective correlatives; and, finally, the work of shaping a canon, as revealed in the overarching structural cohesion of the collection itself. Hitomaro—to whom shrines have been built over the centuries—wrote long and short elegies on the death of his wife that when anthologized in the *Man'yôshû* made literary what had been formulas and incantations. His poetry was a form of rhythmic prose writing. Among his most powerful "long poems" (*chôka*) is one composed, we are told in a headnote to the poem, as an elegy written while grieving the death of his wife. Gazing upon a wild and desolate shore where "vines crawl on the rocks, rockweed of the deep grows on the reefs and sleek seaweed grows," he thinks of his wife, "who swayed toward me in sleep like the lithe seaweed." Unable to master his sorrow, he discovers the sleeves of his "well-woven robe drenched with tears." In keeping with common practice, Hitomaro follows his long poem with two short ones (*tanka*) that distill his emotions into images:

The quick gallop
of my dapple-blue steed
races me to the clouds,
passing far away
from where my wife dwells.

O scarlet leaves
falling on the autumn mountainside:
stop, for a while, the storm
your strewing makes, that I might glimpse
the place where my wife dwells.

In later years, Hitomaro's poetry would be most appreciated as a lost voice of unadorned poetic simplicity and unsophisticated sincerity. Considering the acute rendering of felt pain in this poem about his wife, that is no surprise. What is less frequently noticed, however, is that his poetry was also thoroughly imbued with the art of poetic invention, and that this accounts in large part for its effectiveness in conveying the grief he no doubt sincerely experienced.

Japanese poetry was created in and enabled by a small but open-source culture at court, in which pre-existing writings were reworked and riffed upon. It is a poetic tradition stretching back to the seventh century, born of magical incantation and pre-literate songs and built (after the demise of the long-poem form represented in the *Man'yôshû*) from thirty-one-syllable poems with alternating beats of five and seven syllables that pulsate and are punctuated by literary tropes. It was a poetry written for an expert community of connoisseur court writers and readers.

Within this community, writing combined skillful citations and eloquent echoes. In the best poets, like Hitomaro, individual style and personal voice were not erased, but rendered more visible. What powered this economy of language was barter among the most sensitive and talented, among accomplished readers who were also writers. Japanese poems do not rhyme—the language's limited sound inventory requires other forms of poetic elaboration. Favoring the short form, the poetry has very little to say. So a tradition developed that not only allowed but also demanded skilled allusiveness to the figures of other poems, which in turn depended upon deep reading of the poetry of the past and present. As Fujiwara Teika put it early in the thirteenth century, "There are no teachers in Japanese poetry. We take old poems as our masters. If one seeks inspiration from the old styles and learns one's vocabulary from the great poets of the past, how can one fail to compose good poetry?" In other words, in this kind of literature, the past becomes present not through a transfer of meaning, but through form. And to poeticize well, one was required to have read a lot, and thoughtfully.

One might almost say that a poet of the nineteenth century could read poetry from the ninth century as if it had been written in his or her own time, and that a poet from that earlier time, transported a thousand years into the future, would have no trouble reading that later age's verses. This suggests either a freezing of forms or a limitless pool of poetic play with certain constraints and resonances; and it is the latter that best describes the situation, with its stable, yet infinitely plastic, stock of references and grammar whose deciphering relied on an audience of literate connoisseurs.

A love of wordplay was in part born of necessity from Japanese's spare phonological system, replete with homonyms and near-homonyms. Poetic devices increased the power of language by exploiting the inherent opportunities for play with sounds, meanings, and grammar. These dimensions were further enhanced as a deeply intertextual bent created ripples of unspoken meaning as well, through allusions to famous places, events, and, most importantly, other poems. To weave depth and complexity into the short form required an especially rich menu of resonant and versatile literary devices if the poetry was not to fade away.



And so, from early on, Japanese literature was sustained by the powerful truth that art depends on formal constraint. One constraint was the canon of literary decorum. One expansive response to those constraints was to place the poetry in integrated sequences, or in the back-and-forth gamesmanship of poetic dialogue. Good classical Japanese poetry displayed such technical excellence. But great poetry did not just adhere to these requirements. It deployed technique to produce affecting overtones and evocative resonance: what came to be called *yojô*, a lingering suggestion or aftertaste that would stay with the reader long after the poem ended. Over the centuries, Japanese poetry thus used words, often from the storehouse of pre-existing literature, to register the lyric possibilities of the sensual world and impart to readers a feeling for the mystery of things. In short, it paid verbal tribute to the experience of the ineffable.

The go-to repository of these techniques was the first imperial anthology, the *Kokinshû*, published in 905, although twenty more such imperial anthologies were produced until the last one in 1433. It contains 1,111 poems, and all but nine are thirty-one syllable *tanka*. There are two prefaces, one in Chinese (reminding us that the anthology was a creative translation of Chinese Six Dynasties poetry) and one in Japanese. The chief editor, Ki no Tsurayuki, wishing to distinguish Japanese creativity from the Chinese tradition it had inherited, designated Japanese verse as *uta* or "song," and Chinese verse as *shi* or "poetry" (the term used by the Chinese themselves). This grounding of the Japanese in singing was to have many ramifications.



The most cherished poems from the *Kokinshû* depict the human senses—especially vision and hearing—extending into a world hidden from those very senses, drawing felt-but-unuttered connections between the perceivable and the imperceptible realms. There are no metaphorical leaps from one realm to another, but rather a tracing of connections, a plumbing of the parts of a world just out of reach. Here is Ono no Komachi:

that which fades
its color unseen
the hidden bloom
of the heart
this disenchanted world

The poem speaks to a recognizable existential condition: grief over the pain that comes with loss. But throughout the tradition language play overtook the rendering of emotional states as poem upon poem built upon earlier poem upon poem. Over time, through various kinds of literary techniques (puns, intertextual allusions, variations on moods, themes, diction), language folds deeper into itself. Combining reverence for the tradition with a sense of rivalry with past poets, the *Shinkokinshû* (*New Collection of Poems Ancient and Modern*), published in 1205, drew deeply from and played with the *Kokinshû*'s rhetorical turnings. Such, in fact, was the poets' task—to pull and shape what they could from the past while remaining poetically fertile in the present. The literary technique *honkadori* (an easily accessible allusion to a previous poem) allowed a poet to have the new poem hover between the present and the older poetic world in what was called the "enigmatic style," which evokes a mood of mystery as one poet immerses his poem into the mood of an earlier poem. Literary play, in other words, can lead beyond the literary. Here is Fujiwara Teika:

> Thus it is that the styles of "moving clouds" and "swirling snow"—the snow blown about by the wind, or the spring haze drifting across the cherry blossoms—have an ineffable charm and elegance. A poem that has this indescribable something hovering over it is a superior poem. Such a poem has been compared to a beautiful lady who grieves over something but does so in silence. To say nothing despite one's sadness is impressive. The same thing happens when a little child of two or three brings something to a person, saying, "This, this"—knowing what it wants to say but unable to express itself clearly. The best poems are those that leave something unsaid.

It is as if the poem sounds an echo—a *yojô*—like the traveler's plea to the transient, or like the end whose very elusiveness insists on prolonging the tale. The echo is the carving of a name in the air. The "echo" is, in fact, captured by the critical term *yûgen*—a capacious word inflected variously over the tradition. Formulated by Teika's father, Fujiwara Shunzei, and drawn from Chinese Daoist thought, the term contains two Chinese characters that, respectively, mean faint, dim, and deep, and black, distant, quiet, and occult. Together, the two characters form a term used to describe the transient, yet deeply affecting, character of the echo.

The feeling of *yûgen* gets full treatment in the work of Saigyô, the towering twelfth-century poet. Saigyô has been loved for being simple, direct, and somber. He experienced war and cataclysmic upheavals in the capital city of Kyoto that—to him and many others—spelled foreboding, and an end to all things. Buddhist thinkers at the time reckoned that the end times had come, that the period of *mappô*, begun fifty years before Saigyô's birth, underlay the social chaos of the day. It is this Buddhist sense of temporality that structures Saigyô's poetry, and his lived experience that lends his style a bleak gravity. This style is suggestive of *sabi*—melancholy loneliness—and also draws upon a Buddhist-inflected grappling with attachment and its attendant beauty:

Even free from passions
One could but be moved:
a marsh, a snipe flies up,
an autumn evening



This poem adheres to a common pattern in which vivid images are preceded by a general observation, concluding (in the Japanese) with a noun. Even a person supposed to be detached and free of passion finds, standing before such a scene, what it means to be moved. This all sounds very simple, and the poem can certainly be read that way. But what the translation into English necessarily obscures is the reworking of conventional words and phrases and images that any literate reader of the time would have easily responded to. Through those words, and launching off from some concrete thing in the world (a blossom, leaves, a bell, a seedling), Saigyô takes his poems to the immaterial realm of sound in this twelfth-century synesthetic poem:

The color of blossoms
dyed in sound—
call of the warbler
beyond lovely
spring dawn

The power of *yûgen* to convey the reader from this material world to an enchanted realm beyond would find an even more effective vehicle in the poetry and performance of Nô theater in the fourteenth and fifteenth centuries. Nô created an enveloping aesthetic ambience by bringing together a multiplicity of arts—poetry, narrative, visual design, music, and dance. The aesthetic quality of "profound mystery and grace" (*yûgen*), the highest principle for the Nô actor, would be accomplished through the actor's beautiful postures.

The presentation of the plays offers a rich visual and auditory experience. The plays—originally known as *sarugaku*, or "monkey music"—traditionally begin with staccato horn calls announcing the start of the drama. A brocade curtain is lifted by men with bamboo poles, and a flute-and-drum chorus of eight or ten men enter from one side and sit down, laying their fans down before them. The conventional thud and crack of drums signal the otherworldliness of the play. An actor enters the stage. An actor dissimulated behind his robes and mask, fan in hand, could produce in the audience an intense response to the terrible loneliness of a wandering ghost. The muffled delivery of the text, chanted from the back of the throat; the desolate beat of a drum; the slightest of bodily gestures, all stylized over the centuries and performed by the best actors with virtually no variation; the beauty of the mask and the shadows shifting across it; the design of the costumes and fans: all this captures and performs emotion. Nô is slow, and the most affecting delivery of emotion occurs through the slowest acting and the slowest-moving plots.



Nô is bare and austere and often centers on the theme of death and the eventual deliverance from the mourner's attachment to his own sorrow. It performs these powerful emotions through the most parsimonious means. The stage backdrop is always a stylized pine tree; there may also be indications of a boat, hut, or carriage, stylized as well, and depicted only in outline. The starkness and severity of the set are relieved by the brilliance of costumes set against the barren stage. The slight lifting of a hand toward a slightly lowered mask indicates weeping; painstakingly executed, protracted patterns of movement look like dance: shifting a fan from hand to hand, raising and lowering it at a diagonal, indicates noticing something in the distance. Movement across the stage, which is always as still as possible except in the third act of the play, where movement is frenzied, consists of a slide and the gentlest lift of the foot.

The core of the Nô canon (some six thousand plays written since the fifteenth century) comprises those dozens of plays written by Zeami Motokiyo in the fourteenth and fifteenth centuries. For Zeami, who—as an actor, poet, troupe leader, and theoretician—was the greatest figure in Nô history, the rhythmic chanting of the librettos by singers situated apart from the stage was vital to its aesthetic and affective power. The librettos combine prose and verse. The verse moves at a 5-7 beat, as does all classical Japanese poetry, and is chanted according to the composition at a variety of tempos and pitches. A poetic rhythm of *jo-ha-kyû*—introduction, agitated development, and frenzied closure—guides the narrative as a whole as it does each section of the play, including the gestures of the actors. Achieving the desired response of the audience depends on this rhythm, both heard and seen.

Nô was a theater of *yûgen*, dark, mysterious, and graceful. It was an aristocratic art. Zeami himself was patronized by the military aristocracy, as was Nô for five hundred years (although many Nô plays in the generation after Zeami begin to shade into popular entertainments and were performed at temples and shrines for everyone to see). A theorist of his art whose central goal was to move his audience, Zeami analyzed what for him was the heart of Nô, the art of acting, through images and symbols. This "art of the flower of mystery" can "be symbolized by the phrase, 'In Silla at midnight the sun is bright.' It is impossible to express in words or even to grasp in the mind the mystery of this art. When one speaks of the sun rising at midnight, the words themselves do not explain anything; thus, too, in the art of Nô, the *yûgen* of a supreme actor defies our attempts to praise it."

The play librettos themselves, musically notated, are literary masterpieces, studded with quotations from the classics, written centuries earlier. The dances, too, are keyed to the words and music. It is as if we are at the heart of the Japanese literary imagination, where the reverberations of words, rather than their meaning, make the world.

One of Zeami's most famous plays, *The Shrine in the Fields* (*Nonomiya*), is drawn from two scenes in the eleventh-century *The Tale of Genji*, the great masterwork of the prose tradition and already a classic for two hundred years by Zeami's time. The play is about Lady Rokujô, coldly abandoned by the hero of the work, Prince Genji. Her spirit haunts the novel and kills both a wife and a lover of Genji. In the play, she awaits forlorn at the lonely shrine for her last meeting with her former lover, as depicted in the novel. The play quotes freely from the novel and follows much of the advice of manuals that instruct how to work them into verse poetry. It replays the events in alternating among the chants of the ghost of Rokujô (referred to as the Consort), a wandering monk who seeks her identity, and a chorus that sets scenes, narrates, and also ventriloquizes her words and thoughts as she dances.



In a Nô play, quotations of Japanese poetry, Chinese poetry, Buddhist texts, *The Tale of Genji*, and, most of all, the military epic *The Tale of Heike* could be counted on for immediate recognition by a literate audience. The words are chanted, each syllable of text marked for its vocal rising and falling, for its movement from declaration to recitative to full voice, for the amount of time a sound should be held. The prose portions, about one-third of the plays, are not marked musically and are declaimed in regular cadences. There are fixed rhythms and free rhythms, and three basic structures: a majestic, regular beat, each beat tied to a syllable; a fast rhythm linking one beat to two syllables; and a third distributing twelve syllables across eight beats. The rhythms are flexible, not metronomic, and regularity is studiously avoided.

Then there is the music: a flute that can sustain a melody but sounds both disembodied and ethereal; small and large drums; and cries from the musicians before some beats. The movement of the actors, their dance, sometimes is no more than a stately and slow circling of the stage. Sometimes it is so slow and so apparently lacking in choreography it seems not to be dance at all. This studied slowness is how Nô theater is performed today, but we note that diaries that come to us from Zeami's time tell us that the plays were performed at twice the pace.

Nô enacts a mimesis of subjective feeling rather than of external reality, an imitation of emotion that creates a feeling of mystery, beauty, and power. But the plays did not shy away from bringing to bear the signifying substance of language. Zeami's literary expression was embellished with allusion and peppered with instances of wordplay inherited from the poetic tradition. The prose segments of the librettos served to slacken the tension of the poetry, incorporating mournfully prolonged vowels and formal grammatical endings for percussive effect.



Nô, in short, is where some of the strongest Japanese literary impulses lead: grounded in words while enlisting extra-literary means to enchant viewers and listeners to a place beyond words. Projecting a panoply of forms and surfaces, it evokes an enchanted spirit beyond this world. Nô performs reality through art.

The tension between writing from life and writing from literature, and also between the concrete and the ethereal, is most fruitfully realized in the poetry of Matsuo Bashô, the canonical seventeenth-century haiku poet and writer of prose who is to this day a household name. In a world of writers and literary texts subject to multiple close readings and rereadings over many centuries, none has been written about more. Bashô brought to perfection what would soon become the internationally recognized—and practiced—poetic form, the haiku. (Although Bashô is now most renowned for his "haiku," he was first and foremost a practitioner and teacher of the ancient form of *renga* or linked-verse sequences.) A poem made of three measures of five, seven, and five beats, and always including a "seasonal word" indicating the season depicted in the poem, the haiku did not begin its life as an independent form. Rather, it was originally the starting verse (*hokku*) in a round of *renga*, the most widely composed poetic genre between the thirteenth and sixteenth centuries. The word "haiku" itself did not enter general circulation until well after Bashô's time, when it was used by the poet and critic Masaoka Shiki in the early twentieth century.

Bashô also created a new prose style, *haibun* (haiku-inflected prose), which can be seen in works like the iconic 1694 *The Narrow Road to the Deep North*, where short, crisp, sentences move through poetic associations punctuated by the briefest of poems. Bashô's masterworks from the end of the seventeenth century have earned him renown as a travel writer almost mystically able to capture brilliant snapshots of nature that, at the same time, also reveal the poet's epiphanic experiences. Bashô crystallized Japanese poetry's dual attention to the here-and-now and the otherworldly, through words that were enveloped in words but also reached toward the lingering tone beyond words.



Of his thousand extant poems, the most iconic reveal a quality of *sabi*, a sad loneliness. For Bashô, *sabi*—a term with a history of malleable meanings well predating him—"is the color of the poem. It does not necessarily refer to a poem that describes a lonely scene. If a man goes to war wearing stout armor or to a party dressed up in gay clothes, and if this man happens to be an old man, there is something lonely about him. *Sabi* is something like that."

In this particularly famous poem, loneliness is also a state of quietness:

Still—
A cicada's cry
  Seeps into rocks

Each of the following Bashô poems leaves sound quietly drifting in the ear:

The sound fades,
The scent of the flowers arise
  The evening bell

Old pond—
Frog jumps,
  Sound of water

The brevity of the poems allows an entire verse to be structured around a single sound in the world. This became a primary technique of Bashô and his followers. Each of the poems evokes the experience of a concrete scene in a moment in time. Each refers to an indefinite quality through a definite thing. Bashô was a student of Zen Buddhism and was attentive to such toggling between the concrete and the mystical. His art evoked a something hovering just beyond the concrete world but tied to it, something just graspable but immediately lost—something whose transience we sense and suffer for, something sounded out through words that become music. Bashô believed that stanzas should be linked to each other through fragrance, reverberation, semblance, flow, fancy, or some such indefinable quality.

Bashô's poetry was informed by his Buddhist sensibility as well as by his reading of the classics of Japanese and Chinese poetry. His language is saturated with literary precedents. In the opening of his 1691 *Saga Diary*, he sits in a room gazing upon his books: the eighth-century Chinese poet Bai Juyi's collected poems, Chinese poems by Japanese poets, *The Tale of Genji*, and the early tenth-century *Tosa Diary*. Writing from life did not require leaving one's room.

By the time the practice of haiku reached Masaoka Shiki at the end of the nineteenth century, it was thought to have lost its vigor. He sought to revive it through the concerted practice of "sketching from life" (*shasei*), a totemic literary term and rallying cry, borrowed from European painting by modernizers of literature rallying toward a transparent language that would supposedly record life as it is. In a break with traditional poetic practice, the poet was not to work intertextually, but to minutely observe and record the world. In 1889 Shiki was reading Herbert Spencer's *The Philosophy of Style* and finding in it an argument for the brevity of haiku, which Shiki was studying with an elder poet, having been taught to read and write Chinese poetry since a child.

Shiki criticized Bashô for not rigorously "writing from life," for spiritualizing his poetry by having it lift off from this world into an ethereal beyond and thereby making versifying a sort of religious practice. But Shiki did recognize Bashô's greatness (he thought him to be the only serious poet born since the eighth century) in his ability not so much to register the world by recording the poet's sensations, as to stir the *reader's* sensations through the *poet's* skillful plying of purely literary worlds. Like Bashô, Shiki sought a poetry that through the object of investigation would evoke an immaterial resonance beyond the material.

Writing from life did not mean clinging to things, and poetry was not meant to *mean* anything beyond what it shows. Here is his own accounting of why he loved Bashô's "The old pond / A frog jumps in / Sound of water": "The meaning of the verse about the old pond is nothing more than what appears on the surface.... With respect to the meaning, there is no need to add the slightest particle to the fact that he heard the sound when a frog jumped into an old pond. Anything added to the poem would not be the truth of the haiku about the old pond. This is absolutely clear. The special feature of this poem is that it hides nothing, covers nothing, does not use the slightest artifice, contains not one ambiguous word."

Bashô's poetry creates through sound and vibrations a world of words that reaches beyond words. Its brevity gives it an epiphanic punch. That is what makes it a monumental achievement in the tradition. Shiki works toward the same glittering realm beyond the quotidian through words filtered only by the individual poet's consciousness: "A red apple / A green apple / On top of the table" simply records what is there and has the things themselves reverberate beyond the material world; "I eat a persimmon / and a bell starts booming—Hôryûji." The line moves us in a timeless flash from consciousness to taste to lingering sound.

Masaoka Shiki preached the gospel of writing directly and concretely, a gospel whose source was the poetics of the *Man'yôshū*. Since that time, he thought, Japanese poetry had stagnated. It took its first decisive dive in the finicky poetry and aesthetics of Ki no Tsurayuki, as Shiki bluntly put it in his 1898 polemic, *Letters to the* Tanka *Poets*: "Tsurayuki was a bad poet and the *Kokinshû* is an insipid collection. I would like to tell you that the veneration lavished upon both of them is beyond my comprehension, but I must confess that, until a few years ago, I too venerated the *Kokinshû*. During this time, I thought that Japanese poems (*uta*) embodied elegance (*yûbi*), and that the *Kokinshû* was an anthology of the best verse. Yet now I feel angry and regretful over this; it is as if I had been in a three-year love affair only to wake up one morning and realize that I was being played all along by some disreputable woman."

Shiki strove to avoid all clever wordplay and write directly from life, as he felt Hitomaro did in the *Man'yôshû*. Shiki is a major figure in the tradition because he wagered that a transparent style of sketching from life would be his version of tapping into *kotodama*—the magical power of words—to capture the thing in itself as well as the beyond that the thing reaches toward. Extraordinary it is, then, to witness the great reversal of literature and life that came to Shiki in his final days. Largely bedridden for much of his final six years, in his final days he was wracked with pain and anguish, soothed somewhat by morphine. His world had shrunk to *A Six-Foot Sickbed*, as his journal of the time was titled. In those final days Shiki grappled to find words that could record the immediacy of sensation, as in this, one of his most famous poems:

My teeth stick
Into a ripe persimmon—
Down my beard it drips

In these final days, Shiki transformed the spirit of "sketching from life": from a transparent recording through words of the observed world to a rendering of mental and physical states not dependent on observation: "These days my favorite pleasure is to sketch from life after taking morphine."

Experienced from his sickbed through a shroud of pain, the outside world has all but disappeared and has been dissolved into Shiki's sketches and words. There is no nature; there is only the artist's mental and bodily state, rendered accessible to others through the medium of art.

Shiki's recounting of the decline of Japanese poetry begins with its abandonment of the sincerity of vision of the "long poem" (*chôka*) after its flourishing in the *Man'yôshû*, and its replacement by the pyrotechnic, artificial quality of the classical "short poem" (*tanka*). As he tells it, Ki no Tsurayuki's tenth-century preface to the *Kokinshû* set this quality in stone by claiming that people wrote poetry when moved by phenomena, and by promoting the idea that nothing more than a single impression needed to be recorded.

# Chapter 2
# *The Tale of Genji*

In the first decade of the eleventh century, Murasaki Shikibu, a lady-in-waiting at the imperial court, began writing what was to become the most influential work in the Japanese tradition and, to some, the world's first novel. The novelist Kawabata Yasunari, for example, looking back at the entire Japanese literary tradition, situated Murasaki Shikibu's *The Tale of Genji* at its apex, a view that is widely shared. *Genji* may be the greatest achievement of all of Japanese literature, and has inspired a vast machinery of interpretation, translation into both modern Japanese and other languages, and adaptation in a range of media, throughout the centuries.

*Genji* recounts the sufferings of women at the hands of men, and it is a work darkly enchanted. *Genji* begins with a shining figure, the Radiant Prince Genji. It shows Genji's own disillusionment with a world of beauty and erotic attachment and tracks the disenchantment of the world around him. As his own light dims and eventually dies, the magic of the world of the novel also evaporates, and the novel continues for many chapters describing a world of sere realism. The power of words to effect deep feeling, to ignite love, to dazzle readers both within the world of the novel and without—simply goes away.

Although frequently invoked as a kind of primal ancestor in her own right, Murasaki Shikibu herself was heir to three centuries of evolution in the art of literary narrative. Since the eighth-century *Man'yôshû*, brief prose passages had been used primarily to set the context for poetry; in the tenth century the ratio between poetry and prose shifted, and prose took on a more central role in the genres of the "poem-tale" (*uta monogatari*), and the "poetic diary" (*uta nikki*).

*The Tale of Genji* represents an immense literary leap beyond the poem-tale and the poetic diary. At a length of well over one thousand pages in English and including 795 poems (Murasaki wrote nearly all of them, making her not only a great prose writer but also one of the most prolific poets) it features hundreds of characters, multiple plots and subplots, small and large narrative arcs, explorations of various mental and emotional states, and a self-conscious theory of literature and of the relationship between art and life.



Serious scholarship on *Genji* commenced in the twelfth century. It was a central text for the study of poetry for eight hundred years. But it was only in the eighteenth century that an urban, mercantile reading public turned the work into an object of popular interest, even as its language by then seemed archaic and its contents less often read than heard about secondhand or encountered through its retelling in popular adaptations and parodies. Around that same time, *Genji* also became an object of hermeneutical analysis. Scholarly commentary, a genre dating back to the twelfth century, began to proliferate around the more obscure passages in the book, elucidating every aspect of its style: allusions, pronunciation, and sources. In the seventeenth century, the extraordinary philologist, close reader, and hermeneutic thinker Keichû, a Buddhist priest, plumbed its depths and elaborated through it a science of philology. And its greatest theorist, Motoori Norinaga, found in it the substratum of Japanese thought, feeling, and creativity obscured too long by the dross of Chinese influence.

*Genji* has been parodied by novelists and translated multiple times into modern Japanese, as well as scores of other languages (indeed, there exist today five different translations in English alone). The centuries have seen, too, the appearance of digests, dictionaries, and annotations. *Genji* seems almost infinitely reproducible, across all media—in Nô theater, modern novels, pornography, films, manga, anime, and video games.

However, these signs of unalloyed praise should not obscure its mixed past. Its author, and the art of fiction itself, were condemned so often and vociferously that by the end of the twelfth century, aristocratic women came to offer prayers for the salvation of Murasaki's soul: by writing fiction, she lied, and so, by the lights of Buddhism, she went to hell. A thirteenth-century Nô play consigned Murasaki to a place in hell and depicted prayers being offered for her salvation. Not that Murasaki didn't know what she had coming. In the novel itself, she even pre-emptively orchestrates a conversation in defense of fiction. Fiction, she explains, is a Buddhist *hôben*—a means for achieving salvation—with roots going back to the 100 BCE Sanskrit Lotus Sutra, a text that had long been circulating in Chinese translation and would permeate the literature of her time and after.



*The Tale of Genji* is about longing and jealousy. Genji enters the novel with the loss of his mother and soon afterward finds himself in love with a woman who resembles her: his father's consort, Kiritsubo. The rest of the long tale can be read as a playing out of his erotic transferences, his search for replacements. Longing destroys Genji, as it does many of the women he encounters. The tale becomes progressively more complex, subtle, and psychologically persuasive as it progresses. Genji begins as a perfect hero, as in a romance, and ends as a flawed and even bitter man, as in a novel.

By killing off his mother before we even have a chance to meet her, Murasaki sets the novel—and its structuring patterns—in motion.

By making Genji an orphan, by removing the hand of a powerful mother figure, she makes room for him to develop as a fully realized person with an inner being. We are thus able to witness Genji's hesitations and prevarications. We see him in solitude. We sense his private thoughts and feelings. He has come to seem to many readers to be a person who can leave the page.

*The Tale of Genji* begins not only with illness, death, and longing, but also with beauty, in a darkening world still lit by a flawed-but-enchanting Radiant Prince, whose ascent through courtly ranks will be mirrored by his descent into emotional turmoil and the slackening of his powers to charm both women and his social world. The narrator, sometimes omniscient and sometimes not, reveals the complex and subtle workings of a world structured by desires achieved and thwarted, by the aesthetic art of seduction, by the depredations of women caused by the sexual advances and impositions of men. This is a world saturated by eavesdropping and gossip, of peeping through lattices and thicknesses of clothing and the perfume of objects of longing and lust. To modern eyes at least, our "hero" can appear as an obsessive stalker and self-pitying drama queen who leaves women pregnant and abandoned. Yet, his beauty makes him erotically interesting to both men and women; and his sensitivity toward the sufferings he causes—he is a great poet of life, in this way—redeems him in the eyes of many of the people in his world.



And so it goes, as the reader finds herself rocked between sympathy and antipathy for the Shining Prince. Any compassion we might feel for Genji in his desire to leave the world of desires, in his yearning to sever his earthly ties in the Buddhist fashion, is subtly undercut by the drumbeat of his ostentatious declarations to do just that; any concern we have for his troubles is mitigated by the ease with which he reaches for the most convenient of excuses: karmic fate—the ever-available Buddhist justification for what might otherwise look like irresponsible behavior.

> Genji was experiencing a deep melancholy at the evanescence of the world—an unpleasant realm he dearly wanted to escape. But the birth of his son brought with it obligations that bound him to this world as securely as the ropes used to fetter the legs of horses. He considered renouncing the world—he had been longing to take religious vows for some time—until he was suddenly reminded of another pressing obligation, his little Murasaki, the young lady residing in the west hall at Nijô, who was likely feeling lonely and pining for his return.

In moments like this Genji almost earns our sympathy. However one feels about him, he strikes us as a real, suffering person. But here's what puts *The Tale of Genji* at the heart of the tradition: the reader of *Genji* would be hard put to find moments when her feeling of Genji's felt humanity is not mediated, shaped, and filtered by Murasaki's pointed, frequent reminders that he, like us, is fully absorbed in, and by, art.



Indeed, there is little separating artifice and nature. Notice in the following passage the affiliation between nature and culture:

> The intermittent soughing of the wind in the pines mingled with the indescribably polished sound of forty musicians playing in the shade of tall trees in autumn foliage. Truly it sounded like a breeze blowing down from the deepest mountains, and amidst the multihued leaves that had fallen all around, the dazzling performance of "Waves of the Blue Sea" was sublime. The autumn leaves that had adorned Genji's headdress at the outset had dropped off as the dance proceeded. Having lost a little of its luster, the headdress was now suffering in comparison with Genji's lambent face. So the Consultant who was conducting the musicians of the Left plucked some of the chrysanthemums that'd been placed in front of the Emperor and inserted them into the headdress.

The heart of the scene is not nature "out there" but the experience of sublimity created by the combination of a breeze and a performance. Refreshing Genji's headdress with a flower, readjusting the aesthetic relationship between his luminous face and its surrounding, the conductor of the performance ensures that Genji himself remains a natural work of art.

Reading *Genji*, we experience what much of Japanese literature makes us experience: strong emotions pulsating out of people and

**2. Like the omniscient narrator of the *The Tale of Genji*, in this painting we espy an intimate scene, our eyes gliding past openings in cloud-shaped fields of gold, through spaces left by absent rooftops. Genji, black and white with the briefest glances of color, sits; Murasaki, his object of passion, bows before him in a flowing field of pattern and color.**

things in the world, which do not themselves feel like people and things in the world. The difference is that, in *Genji*, the reader is ever being reminded of that fact, in ways both subtle and explicit. These objects of compassion are, we are reminded when we read attentively, figures of literature, given to us in language that refers to literature. Seduction in particular happens through texts, as lovers or potential lovers or ex-lovers exchange poems that themselves communicate only indirectly, through the skein of poetic language.

In the following courtship scene, making love and making poetry coincide.

> Genji stood uncertainly, hesitating before finally saying a few words of courtship. The lady, however, had been determined not to allow her relationship with him to become as intimate as this, and so she grew sullen and depressed, displaying a cold disposition that signaled she would not permit him to have his way.
>
> *She's getting above herself with these superior airs....*



Genji, we soon learn, can here conjure the woman he desires only through hearing the sounds of a *koto*, a sound created by the movement of silk across the strings rather than by human agency. Nature and artifice, once again, are one. The lovemaking of courtship provides the content for literary play:

> A curtain close by rustled and one of the silk streamers decorating it brushed lightly across the strings of a *koto*. The faint notes conjured to Genji's mind a pleasant image of the lady plucking the instrument, looking relaxed and unguarded. "Is this the *koto* I've heard so much about?" He asked her this and many other things besides, trying to persuade her to play.
>
> *If there were someone I could talk to*
>
> *Intimately, would I awaken*
>
> *from the dream that is this world of woe.*

She replied:

*Wandering just as I am, lost in the darkness*
*Of a night without end, how could I speak to you*
*Not knowing what is dream, what is reality.*

The mood of courtship is darkened by past attachments:

> The dignified bearing of her figure, which he could barely make out in the dim light, put him very much in mind of the Lady at Rokujô, who was now in Uji with her daughter.

The ingress to grief is allowed only by the work of art.

> While he was speaking, Fujitsubo quietly passed away like a flame flickering and dying out. He was overwhelmed by a sadness beyond the power of words.

Grief provides the palette for painting what looks to be a natural scene. But it is Genji who orchestrated the view:

> He had the blinds rolled up, and moonlight streamed into every corner of the chamber, bathing it in a uniformly whitish glow. The poor withered plants in the garden were sagging beneath the weight of the snow, the burbling of the garden stream sounded as if it were sobbing in grief, and the ice on the pond was indescribably desolate. Genji sent the page girls out into the garden to roll snowballs, the adorable figures and haircuts of the younger girls glistened in the moonlight.... The atmosphere was charming.

By having the blinds rolled up and the moon stream in, Genji dabs the image with girls in the garden and then steps back to look and have his aesthetic experience.

Genji's death well into the novel changes the palette of the novel. "With Genji's radiance extinguished, not one among all of his descendants shone with the same glorious light." In the ensuing final chapters, we are with the desolate princess Ukifune (her name means "floating boat"), the beloved of Genji's purported son, Kaoru, and his grandson, Niou. Broken, Ukifune lives on as a nun, in aimless wandering. With the extinction of ardor so goes the power of beauty:

> Kaoru had been waiting in nervous anticipation, impatiently wondering when the boy would return. But as soon as he was informed of Ukifune's vague, uncertain response, a desolate chill settled over him, his ardor cooled, and he concluded that it would have been best to have never sent the letter at all.
>
> Then, another thought occurred to him: *Is it possible someone else is keeping her hidden away?*



What are we reading when we read *Genji*? A reconstruction of episodic narratives originally read to listeners from picture scrolls and then read serially; a work whose earliest extant glimmerings are no more than fragments accompanying a twelfth-century picture scroll; a long narrative whose authoritative versions began being produced at the end of that century, close to two hundred years after its composition; a work that for centuries was read as a sourcebook of poetry and its allusions, and which was finally printed and disseminated to a public readership in the seventeenth century, requiring accompanying commentary to render the language intelligible, and still disseminated mostly in truncated, digest form; and from the beginning of the twentieth century a work finally read as a whole (though still accompanied by commentary and, often, a translation into modern Japanese), and published in free-standing renderings into modern Japanese by novelists.

The Japanese literary tradition has commonly been called a lyric one, poetry being its foundation: forms of romantic communication between lovers that crystallize and intensify feelings. But *Genji* is a brilliant long prose text first and foremost. In early editions, the poetry itself was formatted such that it was barely distinguishable from the prose on the page, flowing calligraphically within it, made distinct only by its prescribed 5-7-5 beat pulse. Centuries of philological, exegetical, and critical labor have gone into making *Genji* what it looks like today: a novel, manifesting a tradition that values a prose realism punctured by lyric moments.

In the eighteenth century, Motoori Norinaga made possible an aesthetically unified, novelistic reading of *Genji*. For Norinaga, *Genji* was the cornerstone of an overarching Japanese poetics, and Norinaga's readings of the novel have since colored all reading of Japanese literature—and many of its clichés—to this day. Twentieth-century readers continue to read by the lights of Norinaga, who found in *Genji* a feminine, intuitive, intrinsically Japanese sensitivity to the beauty of sadness, to the ever-fading quality of things, *mono no aware*.

Norinaga was the first major Japanese theorist of prose fiction (Murasaki herself only inserts discussion on the nature of fiction in her novel). He distanced *Genji* from its Buddhist and Confucian readings and fully secularized the text by arguing that it is governed by emotional sensitivity. Norinaga saw in the emotive efficacy of literature the power to restore the godly nature of those susceptible to being moved by it. That same emotive efficacy would also restore the godly nature (in the Shinto sense of the divine and semidivine beings that populate all of creation) to those who could be likewise moved by reality itself. From this perspective arose his sense of what we might call inter-subjectivity. He spent thirty years deciphering the *Kojiki* (the eighth-century collection of Japanese origin myths) and found there, in the dialogue between the twin founding gods of the Japanese archipelago, Izanami and Izanagi, the earliest example of *mono no aware*, the melancholy, sensitive awareness of the pathos of all things passing. For Norinaga, this was the key to understanding the genre of the tale. It demanded close reading and attunement to feeling, sparking empathy for the fictional characters and leading to the formation of an ethical community in the world.

For Norinaga, Japanese poetry in contrast enacts *mono no aware*. It is language that performs an emotion but does not refer to anything. Poetry is a sigh; and the *monogatari* is an extended sigh. *Genji*'s story of love and jealousy and the anguish of unfulfilled desire is but a prop for staging *mono no aware*. The reason the story narrates the sorrow of repressed or forbidden desires is that only such sorrow produces powerful literature; joy simply would not. And words only become literary when they are fueled by strong emotion.

This argument for a language that performs emotion on the scaffolding of representation echoes Norinaga's critical predecessor Ki no Tsurayuki, who argued eight centuries before for a balance between authentic feelings (*kokoro*) and proper literary words (*kotoba*). This sense of balance makes it possible for Japanese poems to function both purely formally and also as authentic expressions of emotion. Norinaga cherished this balance as well, believing that in his own age of linguistic degeneration, it was already lost.

The thirst for a linguistic and literary revival was strong in Norinaga's time. Norinaga fabricated a chapter from *Genji*, and the novelist Ueda Akinari invented a lost book of the *Man'yôshû*. The criterion of originality as we understand it now did not pertain; writing from within the world of other writings was a practice embedded deep in the cultural sinews. An interest in the art of forgery suggests that, for many writers of that era, simply dipping into the well of accumulated language could slake that thirst and revive the power of literature.

In *Genji*, that degeneration, that melancholy cast, that *aware*, was framed in Buddhist terms, Norinaga's efforts notwithstanding. It is Buddhism that provides its characters with their language of desire, love, seduction, guilt, and regret. "It was our karma" was not an uncommon nor ineffectual pass. Sensitivity to the evanescence of things makes Genji himself an attractive lover—and an annoying self-rationalizer of his bad actions. A Buddhist sensibility also provides some of the structuring principles of the novel. The gradually fading of its world is attributable to its being in its final days, or *mappô*. The narrative's pulsing rhythm of longing, attachment, and loss accords with Buddhism's fundamental truths. In short, Buddhism allows us to make sense of the way in which the novel begins with Genji's brilliant glow, which begins to fade almost as soon as it appears, and which concludes in a blanched everydayness.

*Genji* is also a novel that lets the reader know that it is about nothing more than literature itself. But it knows that, by letting the reader know that it knows this, it can produce the illusion of a transparent view onto reality. Aware as well of its own distrust in the value of words, a distrust that is rooted in the Buddhist notion that words are illusory markers of a phantom reality, the novel only trusts words to perform artistically, to be words about other words. From behind this net it allows to emerge a feeling of reality, of intense jealousy or longing; through this net we hear the whispers of a given character speaking to him- or herself, and perhaps most of all the inner, confused musings of the fractured, troubled conscience of its main character, Genji.

It is thus that we are enchanted by the power of words, by *kotodama*, to remake the world. The invented emotions of a fictional person, created whole cloth from layers of literary allusion and precedent, make us feel the reality of his inner and outer worlds. There are long pauses in the novel for explicit discussions of the nature and value of fiction. In addition to the scenes of lovemaking (in the old-fashioned sense), the novel is occupied with scenes of connoisseurship, not only of literature and art and music, but also of human beauty and the gestures of style. The world, it seems, is available only as an object of artistic judgment. The novel is utterly self-conscious about its being a made-up story, even as it seems a realistic depiction of court life—and was certainly read as such.

Kawabata Yasunari was one among many of Japan's most imaginative writers who sought new elaborations of novel writing by dipping back into *Genji* for inspiration. But *Genji* itself invited elaboration and emendation as, for almost a millennium, writers have engaged in the art of filling in its perceived gaps, writing "missing" chapters. Even the Belgian novelist Marguerite Yourcenar wrote one. And then there is the never-ending work of interpretation and translation. The novel has been subjected to countless interpretations. *Genji* scholarship is more than a cottage industry; it is an empire in Japan. It has been translated more than once into modern Japanese: three times by the novelist Tanizaki Jun'ichirô (who also wrote *The Makioka Sisters* [1948], a novel-of-manners modeled on *Genji*, set among the 1940s Osaka merchant class), and twice by the renowned poetess Yosano Akiko.



*Genji* would become a world of words nurturing other worlds of words. In the twelfth century, Fujiwara Shunzei wrote that it was to be regretted that any poet would compose without having read *The Tale of Genji*. Shunzei was referring to the intertextual practice of making poems out of scenes from past prose narratives. Here is a poem (one of the most celebrated in the entire tradition) by his son Teika that does just that, and, by doing so, evokes the atmosphere of lingering overtones (*yojô*) and ethereal beauty (*yôen*) of the final chapter of *Genji*, "The Floating Bridge of Dreams." Beautiful in its own terms, the poem is only enriched by its allusion to the great classic.

The spring night of
the floating bridge of dreams
has broken away:
drifting away from the peak,
a sky of trailing clouds.

*Genji*'s gift to the tradition was prodigious. Ihara Saikaku's 1682 novel, *The Life of an Amorous Man*, was modeled on *Genji*, rewriting in its own fifty-four chapters the fifty-four chapters of *Genji*. Saikaku established a new genre of realistic, humorous fiction that described all forms of erotic interaction, across and between genders, and often reads like a catalogue of sexual mores and practices. In Saikaku sexual potency stands for poetic potency. In 1680 he composed 4,000 linked poems in a single day, and after publishing *Life of an Amorous Man* went on to write 23,500 in one shamanistic performance. The hero of *The Life of an Amorous Man*, modeled after the character Genji, devotes his life to satisfying all forms of sexual desire. His model in this was Ariwara no Narihira, the tenth-century court poet who was mythologized as the quintessential sensitive poetic lover. Medieval commentaries put the number of his lovers at 3,733. Saikaku's hero surpassed him for a total of 3,742 women and 725 men.



For the novelist Enchi Fumiko, in her 1956 novel *Masks*, *Genji* is the source of feminine power, a playbook for a scorned woman who channels the idea of spirit possession to instigate a plot of revenge. Enchi suggests that the emotional core of *Genji* is not, despite its name, Genji himself, but one of his earliest spurned lovers, the Lady Rokujô, whose anguish knows no surcease and whose ghost haunts Genji and his other women even after her death. In *Masks*, a female *Genji* scholar argues for Murasaki's proto-feminism and Lady Rokujô's embodiment of the archetype of men's eternal fear. She explains:

> Murasaki Shikibu's modernism is evident here in the skeptical view she takes of the medium's powers (although exorcism was in her day an established practice), and in her perception that what is taken for possession by a malign spirit might in fact be the working of the victim's own conscience.... She was able to combine women's extreme ego suppression and ancient female shamanism, showing both in opposition to men.

A greater measure of *Genji*'s influence, or at least evidence of its enduring presence as a deep undercurrent in the Japanese literary prose tradition, is its subterranean, formative power in the works of novelists with no overt links to the world of *Genji* at all: novelists like Nakagami Kenji, who in the 1970s created, in works like *The Cape* (*Misaki*) and *The Sea of Withered Trees* (*Karekinada*), a working-class court of characters caught in webs of family lineage and language. These are novels that combine, like Kawabata Yasunari's novel *Snow Country*, the grit of the daily grind with the sparkle of the otherworldly. They are novels Nakagami hoped to infuse with the magic of the tale, or *monogatari*, whose apotheosis was *The Tale of Genji*.

Nakagami hoped to re-enchant literary language through a new, and very old, kind of narrator and narration. He explicitly called his fictions not "novels," but *monogatari*, which he believed could evoke in its readers that genre's ancient feeling for mystery and the unsayable. Through the form of the tale, Nakagami believed, he would dispense with the modern novel's Aristotelian structure, which begins at a beginning and ends at an end; eliminate the "interior" depths of self, psychology, and meaning below the surface of the modern novel's language; and reject the very idea of the transparency of language. As we might say about *The Tale of Genji*, to Nakagami there was nothing outside the tale: "There is no such thing as the moon; there is only the moon as a tale."

A deep reader of Faulkner, Nakagami created a world like Yoknapatawpha County, a rough-and-tumble construction workers' world on the outskirts of urban life, through which his protagonists grunt and sweat their way through life, struggling to free themselves from the tales of kinship that seem to ordain their fates, like a novel holding sway over its characters. The protagonist of these tales, Akiyuki, explodes that web of language, the tale, and the family lineage it describes, through acts of raw sex, and finally of incest. As *The Cape* opens, Akiyuki, a young construction worker, is immersed in a moment of pure feeling.

He is "soaked in the work site"—a refrain we hear repeated throughout the novel. Akiyuki has moments when his senses merge with the landscape, as if he had stepped out of a Kawabata novel:

> The river was glittering. The blue-green, which flowed within the dark green of the trees growing on the mountain, seemed to Akiyuki like a solitary proof of life and movement. He felt the bright, blue-green water pouring through his own open eyes and then into his veins, and he sensed his body being dyed bright and blue. He often had this feeling—constantly while doing construction work. Sweat would drip from Akiyuki as he dug, and he would feel transformed into the pure motions of digging and scooping, moving with a power he need not think about or evaluate. He obeyed the precise commands of the earth, matching his movements to the hard ground and to the soft. Akiyuki was steeped in the work site. He sometimes suddenly felt that he was masturbating with the earth as his companion.



Constantly digging, Akiyuki is surrounded by musical reverberations: "To Akiyuki doing his work, the landscape steeped in the sun was like music." Akiyuki breathes in nature, and nature reverberates within him like music; he is a flute through which the music plays: "It was merely that Akiyuki himself could not see the Akiyuki who had taken into his now hollow body, his body like the stem of a plant, the music of the rustling of the grasses and the voices of the cicada seeped in the sun."

In a series of essays on the jazz giants John Coltrane, Miles Davis, Thelonious Monk, and Albert Ayler, Nakagami likens the genre of the tale to a musical form in which one creates new chords in order to destroy old ones. This is a form of improvisation that refers to and departs from the earlier imitative improvisatory forms of the poetry in *Genji* and in linked verse. Unlike those earlier revivifying combinations of open-source material, for Nakagami improvisation creates an original voice by destroying all others—like his modern predecessor Akutagawa, Nakagami inches toward originality by imitation. To destroy the tale, one must blow apart all chords; one must play a free jazz like John Coltrane's, which blows to a limit one cannot even sense as a limit, and destroys the chords from which free jazz develops.

Blues, says Nakagami, is like a chanted Buddhist sermon, and it is also like a Nô play, with an introduction (*jo*), an exposition (*ha*), and a furious finale (*kyû*). Music like this is the liberated space of true love, of sorrow, of rage: it is the world of Black Is Beautiful. To him Coltrane's classic "A Love Supreme" is a polystructural and polytheistic rejection of the monotheism of Europe and its attendant system of modernity. Coltrane blows in constant movement in resistance against the center, against linearity, against stasis. This, says Nakagami, is Coltrane's Buddhism. Coltrane blows through the space of Nakagami's fictions—through the *roji*, or alley, as Buddhist chants for salvation do. For Nakagami, a late epigone of Murasaki Shikibu, the word was enchanted through music. That was his form of literary cognition.



To return to another form of literary cognition closer in time to Murasaki and *The Tale of Genji*: Sei Shônagon, the eleventh-century progenitor of the essay form, a fellow court lady-in-waiting and contemporary of Murasaki Shikibu, worked through the tradition's most profound enterprise by exploring the nature of our cognition and representation of the things that inhabit the world. The Japanese literary imagination is many things, but at its core it is rich with the awareness that there is nothing other than literature to mark the presence of the world. It knows that words formally ranged against the world speak the idiom of the senses, but do so in order to address, render, and evoke reverberations beyond words. In common usage words signify things transparently: a "rock" is a rock. Japanese writers, from the beginning, have weaved words together so tightly that they have almost made the world disappear. In the wake of that disappearance words themselves became the stuff of the world.

Reading Sei Shônagon we are swept up into the meandering thoughts and descriptions of a powerful and sensitive narrator. They come to feel that they are passive creatures at the mercy of idiosyncratic moods, impulses, and attachments. They witness both her rage to classify and her art of fragmentation. Sei Shônagon inaugurated a genre comprised of catalogues and lists and aesthetic evaluations—of literature, nature, the social world. Her lists, laced with ironical observations, read like short essays. Her ironic aphorisms and wordplay have been quoted through the centuries. Her seeming randomness has been both critiqued and lauded.

A small sample of Sei Shônagon's lists includes bridges, birds, villages, waterfalls, anthologies, poetic subjects, rare things, things that have a long way to go, things that lose by being painted, things that gain by being painted, things that give a hot feeling, shameful things, winds, islands, beaches, temples, and plain things that give a clean feeling (these are an earthen cup, a new metal bowl, a rush mat, the play of the light on water as one fills a vessel, a new wooden chest). Here is her list of things that make one's heart beat faster:

> Sparrows feeding their young, to pass a place where babies are playing. To sleep in a room where some fine incense has been burnt. To notice that one's elegant Chinese mirror has become a little cloudy. To see a gentleman stop his carriage before one's gate and instruct his attendants to announce his arrival. To wash one's hair, make one's toilet, and put on scented robes; even if not a soul sees one, these preparations still produce an inner pleasure. It is night and one is expecting a visitor. Suddenly one is startled by the sound of raindrops, which the wind blows against the shutters.

We can read Sei Shônagon's lists and brief essays for their content. They are, however, literarily designed. The final passage above is as clear as its own moonlight; it has no pronouns, and it converts readers from witnesses to participants without dipping down into metaphor and association, as in the poetry of her time. We stay with the melody and are pulled by the syntax without moving away. With Sei Shônagon we do not process the poetic code—as would be required by the fancy wordplay of her time—but just register the poetic beauty that lies on the surface of her language.

Sei Shônagon's greatest literary descendent, Yoshida Kenkô, fourteenth-century Buddhist monk, literary essayist, and thinker about aesthetics, wrote what remains one of the masterworks of the tradition, the 1332 *Tzurezuregusa* (*Essays in Idleness*). Kenkô possessed a more pointedly Buddhist imagination than his predecessor. For him, fragmentation of style reflected the impermanence of reality. In the centuries to follow, *Tsurezuregusa* was perhaps the most influential work of style, a handbook for writers like Saikaku centuries later. Kenkô's most known lines concern the aesthetic experience and the rendering of transience: "If man were never to fade away like the dews of Adashino, never to vanish like the smoke over Toribeyama, but lingered on forever in the world, how things would lose their power to move us! The most precious thing in life is its uncertainty. . . ."

Yoshida Kenkô's writing is imbued with the agonies and pleasures of attachment to the transience of things, transience materially embodied in the objects available to the senses. If literature poses the problem of how things impress themselves upon the human sensorium, of how we can come directly in contact with an object, then Kenkô gets right to the heart of the matter. Each and every thing is unreliable because they are impermanent. Language too cannot be relied upon; it once was efficacious but has degenerated: "Nobody is left who knows the proper name of hanging a quiver before the house of a man in disgrace with His Majesty." There yet remains the hope that things, serving as aesthetic prostheses, can generate creative language. "If we pick up a brush, we feel like writing; if we hold a musical instrument in our hands, we wish to play music. Lifting a wine cup makes us crave sake; taking up dice, we should like to play backgammon. The mind invariably reacts in this way to any stimulus. . . . "

Things are out there in the world, but Kenkô sees that we do not need the world to write about them: "Are we to look at the moon and the cherry blossoms with our eyes alone? How much more evocative and pleasing it is to think about the spring without stirring from the house, to dream of the moonlit night though we remain in our room!" The mind is an empty mirror, never projecting onto objects but only receiving them: "Being without color or shape of their own, they reflect all manner of forms. If mirrors had color and shape of their own, they would probably not reflect other things."

The Cuban writer Alejo Carpentier thought that the baroque flourishes of Latin American literature were born of a fear of the void and a desire to fill it. For Kenkô, "Emptiness accommodates everything. I wonder if thoughts of all kinds intrude themselves at will on our minds because what we call our mind is vacant? If our minds were occupied, surely so many things would not enter them." Japanese literature has dwelled easily with what Kenkô calls "emptiness." An empty mind invites into it all things, and the writer transforms those things into words that direct us back to the music beyond words:

> As a rule, the pitch of a bell should be the tone of *ôshiki* [tonic A]. This tone evokes an atmosphere of transience. It was the tone of the bells at the Monastery of Mutability at the Gion Monastery. The bell for the Saionji Temple was cast and recast again and again because they wished it to be in the *ôshiki* tone, but in vain. A bell was eventually found in a distant province. The sound of the bell of the Jôkongô Temple is also in the *ôshiki* tone.

# Chapter 3
# Enchanted realism

That the power of language was in a degenerated condition relative to the past has been the accepted poetic wisdom in every period of Japanese literary history. Lived language was always a shadow of some earlier, more vibrant way of writing. In the 1880s, a modern literary language—a language of realism—was being formed with the by now familiar goal of becoming a transparent medium; but now, its object was the revelation of the alienated modern self. Still, the prosaic quality of realism elicited dismay. How was the beauty of language to be salvaged? How was a writer to create a language that was a pellucid opening to the world of things, but that also reached beyond that world; how could one craft a language that was both quotidian and enchanted? These were perennial challenges throughout Japanese literary history. Where was the new Hitomaro who might forge a language that felt both transparently open to the world but also immersed in literary figuration? Who would take the lead in this new chapter of Japanese literature's search for linguistic transparency in the face of a thick mesh of foreign literatures, hermetic literary forms, and a Buddhist unease with words?

The long and vexed tradition of evoking emotion by mediation through the canon, of never getting directly to the world without recourse to the prism of other writers' words, dissipated finally with the late nineteenth- and early twentieth-century determination to describe a modern world that seemed well out of reach of that canon, however rich its legacy. This urge was aided and intensified as writers delved into the great works of European realism, spurring a generation to wrestle the Japanese language into an idiom that could truly speak to and about Japanese modernity, and to modernity writ large. As a result, their literature provides brilliant snapshots of a language in the process of being transformed: style now would have to look like an absence of style; language would now have to look like it wasn't even there, as if it were dissolving into the reality it conveyed. By the first decade of the twentieth century, what looks more or less like present-day literary Japanese, a plain style, was set in place.

The call to realism was launched by the literary theorist Tsubouchi Shôyô—translator of Shakespeare's entire oeuvre into Japanese between 1884 and 1928—in his 1886 *Essence of the Novel*. In developing a theory of the modern novel, Shôyô called upon a variety of prose styles, from *The Tale of Genji* to nineteenth-century Japanese writers, and from European masters of realist prose to the eighteenth-century novels of Ueda Akinari, one of the greatest prose writers of his time, avidly read by later novelists, adored by Mishima Yukio. Akinari built some of his now classic novels out of the plots of Chinese novels, quoting freely from them, forming his literary worlds through other literary worlds. His *Tales of Moonlight and Rain* (made into a stunning movie by Mizoguchi Kenji) comes from a Nô play featuring as a character another writer, the medieval Buddhist poet Saigyô, and its content and structure draw on the poetic classics. (Akinari wrote studies of Hitomaro and of *Man'yôshû* poetry.) Akinari's literary language was drawn from a wide stylistic palette, intermingling Chinese and Japanese, and blending high and low styles.



The idiom of realism served its purpose and instigated some extraordinary writing. In the hands of the best writers the style was worked into complex, searing, and raw portrayals of the lives of the working poor and allowed for a deep inhabiting of daily life. The twentieth-century master of what might be called a gritty magical realism, Kawabata Yasunari, anointed one such writer, Tokuda Shûsei, as one of the three pinnacles of Japanese literature (the other two being Murasaki Shikibu and the seventeenth-century novelist Ihara Saikaku). Informed by a mixture of Marxist thought, naturalism, and his own experience as a member of what he called the "property-less classes" and a reader of Zola, Maupassant, Dickens, and Hugo, and apprentice to the most popular writer of the 1890s, Ozaki Kôyô, Shûsei wrote hundreds of short stories, novellas, children's stories, and a set of masterpieces of literary fiction. He wrote about class conflict, the new independent woman, and discrimination against the underclass, and he championed what he called "the spirit of prose," issuing a call for prosaic writing to counter the romantic embellishments of state propaganda.



Shûsei created a form of realism that incorporated social realism and popular melodrama, but also experiments in narrative unfolding. His 1925 *Rough Living* was serialized, like many Japanese novels of the time, in a newspaper. The novel frankly treats sexuality, sexual dysfunction, and disease. It reveals the structure of everyday life for working people struggling under capitalism. In this world, time works not in line with the official clock but according to memory: through digression and association. The heroine, Oshima, is an independent and indomitable young woman who fights adversity with delight. She often feels depression and pain, but also joy in her body's vigor. Born to a prosperous family, she evades repeated attempts to be married off, endures bad husbands and lovers, and works toward some success with a common-law husband, whom she eventually abandons for an attractive employee. We watch her as she struggles not to fall into the disrepute of the sex trades. For many chapters, time is marbled by the passing of seasons, nature providing a beautiful and timeless backdrop.

*Rough Living* is very much about the everyday life of nameless urban masses—an inarticulate maid, a woman with a shady past struggling to stay in a respectable neighborhood, or the heroine, a wandering seamstress, Oshima. This is the life of daily drudgery of the laborer, rickshaw puller, and textile worker, always on the verge of disintegration: families fall apart, businesses implode, people barely get by. Oshima moves through failures and successes with her eye on something better. We are swept along by Oshima's memory of herself as a young, uneducated girl who works harder in the fields than the men do, speaks roughly, is threatened with violence by her biological parents, is fostered out, takes multiple lovers and common-law husbands, and longs to escape overseas.

Shûsei is among many Japanese writers who have treated hard labor and poverty. There exists a veritable canon of Marxist and proletarian writers, the best of whom, like the novelist and cultural theorist Nakano Shigeharu, rose above mere agitprop. The very best novelists writing proletarian literature in the 1920s were women—Sata Ineko, Miyamoto Yuriko, Nogami Yaeko, and Hirabayashi Taiko—who produced what would become a small canon of novels, short stories, and political, literary writing about work, poverty, and politics and the toll they took on human relationships.



Shadowing the dominant literary practice of realism was the work of writers resisting the call of the real and the stripped-down style it demanded, writers who continued to work the beauty of the language and valued more the crafting of literariness than the description of new material realities and revelations of modern loneliness, alienation, angst, and upset. Most of these writers engaged in virtual apprenticeships in modern realism before moving on to more flamboyantly literary, and literarily self-conscious, styles (which earned them the reputation among their contemporaries as antiquarians). Their work bespeaks a strong resistance to the idea that writing can or should artlessly reveal the truth of human interiority. A striking example of this opposition can be seen in the active rejection of the novel as a serious literary form by a writer who had mastered it—a writer who lived in Germany, read European literature deeply and with sophistication, and translated some of their masterworks: Mori Ôgai.

Mori Ôgai, a senior medical officer of the Japanese Army, transmitter to Japan of advanced European medical thinking, and translator of Goethe, Schiller, Ibsen, Hauptmann, and Hans Christian Anderson, was a primary progenitor of the Japanese modern novel. In his 1890 novel, *The Dancing Girl*, Ôgai described a young Japanese intellectual sent to Germany by his government to further his studies and take his place among the most elite translators and brokers of European culture and thought, only to fall for a poor dancing girl and suffer the proverbial fate of having to choose between his heart and his intellect, his passion and his duty, his lover and his state.



Ôgai's short novel occupies a central place in the imagination of Japanese literary and political modernization: it is the first and most precisely encapsulating story of the birth of modernity and of the modern self, of that birth's triumphs and sorrows. Two sublime epiphanies structure the story, each showing the hero literally blacking out, yet each leading in a different direction: one toward passion and an intensely felt self, suffering in love, the other toward a surrendering of the individual will to the demands of the state. Together, they yield one notion of the modern Japanese subject: aware of an inner self that suffers but is also socialized to the harmony of the state, in service at its pinnacle to the emperor.

The protagonist of the novella, Ôta, is in Germany to learn the tools of modernization and take them home with him. In a distinctively archaic Japanese literary language, the novel portrays Ôta as lured by the "exceeding beauty" of one Elise, whose room is littered with books by Schopenhauer and Schiller. He draws away from his civic responsibilities, falls in love with Elise, and impregnates her. He is, however, convinced by a compatriot to leave her for home. In the last lines of the story, Ôta curses that friend.

The standard reading of the story is that the hero sacrifices personal love for duty to the state. The affair with Elise was a brief fancy, a fairy tale whose quaint distance from reality was painted in Ôgai's self-conscious use of archaic Japanese. But this decision to return to Japan is less a willed choice than a giving up of the will to a force greater than his besotted self. Ôta loses his object of passion in Germany—along with his mixed-race baby—and awakens ready for work in Japan. Fifteen years later, Ôgai himself would wake from his novelist's slumber when the national hero General Nogi performed the by then very old, anachronistic act of ritual suicide (with his wife) following the death of his lord—the Meiji emperor.

Following these two deaths, Ôgai abandoned the genre of the novel for the rest of his life and wrote biographies of famous men and women and historical narratives that described acts of loyal self-immolation sanctioned by traditional forms, stories in which the only quality of character that mattered was one's proper form, and in which one's self was defined by one's Confucian web of relationships. Needless to say, in these stories there is no revelation of psychological interiority because to Ôgai the self was now simply an illusion: no fictional plotting, no playfulness with narrative point of view, and no irony. For Ôgai, ritual death and the individual enacting it could not be represented in the genre of the novel. In fact, he believed, there is no interior, psychological "self." A person is not his psychology; he is his acts and relationships, and nothing more.

But, having no choice but to accept the inevitability of the reign of realism that could be trusted to transparently render the world and the modern notion of the psychological self, Ôgai nevertheless chose to channel the sanctioned Japanese impulse to regard words mistrustfully. In his 1909 *Vita Sexualis*, a send-up of the novel genre and of Freudian psychoanalysis, Ôgai dismisses the belief that one's internal life can be revealed and cured through narration and the notion that one's essence can be revealed through an exploration of the formation of one's psychology in specific moments of time. His case in point is a certain Mr. Kanai Shizuka, "philosopher by profession" and reader of the greatest Japanese novelist, Natsume Sôseki, Japanese naturalism, Emile Zola, and German sexology. Mr. Kanai has decided to investigate the etiology of his sexual impotence. We read his year-by-year chronicle of erotic development until it breaks off at age twenty-two, when he leaves for Germany to study. Dreaming of his time there after his return three years later, recalling his casual encounters with prostitutes, and cogitating on the nature of his written work, Mr. Kanai has an epiphany: his impotence is better understood to be a conquering of desire, his writing is genre-confused (it is neither autobiography or novel) and has nothing to reveal at all. Let all be consigned to silence. The last lines of Ôgai's novel read: "He picked up his pen and wrote in large letters in Latin across the front cover of his manuscript, VITA SEXUALIS. He heard the thud of his manuscript as he hurled it inside a storage chest for books."

A few years after Ôgai made his farewell to the novel in VITA SEXUALIS, he wrote his first short historical tale, *The Last Testament of Okitsu Yagoemon*, describing a ritual suicide performed in veneration of the emperor. In another such piece, *The Incident at Sakai*, Ôgai narrated the ritual suicides of eleven Japanese soldiers ordered by their superiors to publicly disembowel themselves in compensation for the eleven French soldiers they had killed. The French captain was to witness the event. The meaning of these men's lives is accessible not through an analysis of inner selves that have developed over time, but through simply stating who they are and how they comport themselves. The language chosen for this rendering is not the modern language of realism, designed for a transparent revelation of psychology, but the complex ceremonial language of the nineteenth century.

> Nishimura, who was called next, was a gentle man. His family lineage was Minamoto, his name Ujiatsu. He had grown up in the village of Enokuchi in the district of Tosa. He was born in 1845, and was now twenty-five with the rank of Mounted Escort on an annual stipend of forty *koku*. He had been assigned to the Sixth Tosa Division in the eighth month of 1867. Nishimura took his place on the seat of *seppuku* wearing his military uniform, the buttons of which he carefully loosened one by one. He then took his short sword, thrust it into his left side and began to pull it across to the right; but, as if he thought the penetration too shallow, he drew the blade in deeper before slowly pulling it over to the right. His second Kôsaka seemed a little frightened; even before Nishimura had finished pulling the blade to the right, he struck from behind. The head flew almost six meters.

Ôgai's writing of these scenes looks forward to the novelist (and Ôgai devotee) Mishima Yukio's literal take on *seppuku*, and back to the hybrid Japanese/Chinese prose of Japan's first war-tale, the early eleventh-century chronicle *Shômonki* (*The Rebellion of Masakado*), the story of the rise and fall of the insurgent warrior, Taira no Masakado. Written in a hybrid of Chinese and Japanese, and seamlessly alluding to Chinese precedent, *Shômonki* is very much at ease being betwixt and between the two literatures and histories. Ôgai's work was less so. One of the soldiers in *The Incident at Sakai*, before his own disembowelment, announces that he does so not for the French, but for his emperor. His final performance makes his point: "Because of the depth of the initial thrust, the wound gaped widely. Releasing his sword, Shinoura then placed both hands within the cut and, pulling out his own guts, glared at the French consul."

If in *Vita Sexualis* a visit to the European continent allowed the Japanese writer to reject the modern literary style learned in great measure from European writing, here that rejection is thrust in the face of the European who watches the suicide in horror. Ôgai has relinquished the realism of modern literature and affirmed literature's literariness.

For Ôgai, the quest to create the language of the modern Japanese novel had finally reached a dead end. In the 1890s, Kitamura Tôkoku had already noted that words had been calcified by the language of politics. He argued for a language that went beyond what the eye could see, beyond the reach of modern thought. In seeking to resist the alienating effect of instrumentalist thought, which reduced the self to an abstracting, thinking mind, Tôkoku wrote of a love that bypassed the intellect in its capacity to apprehend the world. Literature, he said, was not a "practical enterprise." Shakespeare, Wordsworth, and the nineteenth-century Japanese novelist Takizawa Bakin were to him "great warriors" who had their sights on "the limitless mysteries of heaven." Their work was "a striking at the clouds and a reaching for the stars." We will see that such an aesthetic position—soothing the thinking mind with the feeling heart—could also fuel a dangerous politics of beauty.

Like Ôgai, some contrarian modern novelists during this time also attempted to counter, through rhythm, what they saw as the grayness of prosaic, utilitarian language shorn of aesthetic flair. Kôda Rohan, for example, strove to approximate the styles and rhythms of pre-modern literary modes that he saw as threatened with extinction by the advent of standardized Japanese in the late nineteenth century. He had also lived with the prose rhythms of the Chinese-inflected style and earlier performative oral narratives. Inheritor of an aesthetically rich tradition, yet dedicated to forging a modern literature, Rohan devoted himself to the project of instilling stirring rhythm into transparently bland prose.

Rohan was a cosmopolitan writer to his very core, a reader of all world literature—Shakespeare, Goethe, the Chinese historian

Sima Qian, and the Chinese poet Du Fu, all of Japan's classics and its popular literature, and also Confucian, Daoist, Buddhist, and Greek thought. For Rohan, the spirit of literary play was still possible in the 1880s, even under the domination of realism. In his 1889 *The Bodhisattva of Elegance*, he wrote in a style that combined colloquial dialogue, neoclassical narrative description, Japanese renderings of Chinese poetry and prose, Japanese readings of Chinese ideographs, and the language of classical Japanese poetry. Later in his career, Rohan undertook an investigation of onomatopoetic words and argued against the dominant notion, in Japan and elsewhere, then and now, that words and sounds are only arbitrarily connected. Words *were* their sounds, Rohan believed, and the world itself was sound, as he wrote in a 1926 story:

> For a long time he thought that the world was boundless, but now he wondered if the world was nothing more than this *zaaaa* and, thinking this through again, if this thing *zaaaa* was, precisely, the world. He felt as if the voice *ogyaa-ogyaa* that he first gave off at birth and the voice *gyaa-tto* made by others and then the entire array of voices created in the various commotions that one makes—the *kyaa-kyaa, gan-gan, bun-bun-guji-guji, shiku-shiku* made when reading books, singing songs, laughing in joy or screaming in anger—and the sounds of a horse neighing, a cow bellowing, a car jolting, a train booming, a steamship churning the waves, and the faint sound of one needle falling on a wooden floor—he felt as if all these, without exception, came together and entered into that sound *zaaaa*; and then if he concentrated and listened quietly, he distinctly recognized that all these various sounds most certainly did exist in the one sound, and while he was thinking that yes, this was the way it was, before he knew it he could no longer hear the *zaaaa*.



Rohan was well aware of the long tradition of the power of non-semantic sound going back to *kotodama*. For the eighth- and ninth-century Buddhist monk, scholar, and poet Kûkai, who founded a major school of Japanese Buddhism, Sanskrit had an elevated stature. Unlike Chinese ideographs, thought to mimic reality, Sanskrit sounds were believed to be generated out of the originary sounds of the universe. In the seventeenth century the philologist Keichû, drawing on Kûkai, wrote that the sound "a" was the origin of all teachings and imbued the semiotics of language with emptiness. Keichû extended this religious potency to all language: Japanese poetry was a mantra meant for Japanese people alone and pointed them to the Buddhist teaching on the emptiness of all things. Japanese poetry's very brevity was precisely what allowed it to reveal the interdependence of all reality. (The twelfth-century poet Saigyô compared composing a poem to creating a Buddhist shrine, or stupa.)

This concept of a sound-based language—a musical language—would indeed come to play a central role in the development of a new kind of literary language in the 1920s and 1930s: one that similarly eschewed the signifying function of language in favor of the musicality of prose, and that sacrificed conceptual or narrative clarity in favor of an abundance of style. The writers who pursued this ideal followed in the footsteps of predecessors in the 1890s, such as Izumi Kyôka, in their desire to resist what, to them, was the dispiriting use of literary language as a blunt instrument of explication. They attempted to work against the commonly held belief that language was a transparent medium by countering it with the aesthetic force of rhythm. For modern writers who loved language *qua* language, the sinuosity of long classical sentences could carry the aesthetic burden. Ishikawa Jun self-consciously drew on eleventh-century Japanese prose, magical realism, and playful—even verbally acrobatic—popular writing from the eighteenth and nineteenth centuries in his sinuous and prolix sentences. Here is the opening of his 1936 *The Boddhisattva*:

> Just as a bead of water upon a lacquer tray glitters and is gone before the hand that would hold it gemlike between two fingertips, so too the curious sparkle of Tarui Moichi dissipates when one

> considers him a potential character in a novel. He is nondescript; and one wonders, with the feeling somehow of being cheated, what had made him seem extraordinary. For the breezes that stir the pages of this novel are far different from the gusts of the mundane worlds, and Moichi too ordinary and insubstantial a subject—to pinch him is to crush him—should we, in taking him up as the topic of our tale, decide to scorn the earth and, by the sheer force of our soaring flight to the heights of seventh heaven, brush from our wings the dust of the floating world and the dregs of human sentimentality.

Such a classically inflected style, kept alive and reinvented by modernists, allowed for the easy capture of the style of James Joyce's *Ulysses* when it was translated in the 1970s. In the 1980s, the novelist Nakagami Kenji enacted his own reclamation of that earlier classical style in the endlessly meandering prose of his 1982 *A Thousand Years of Pleasure*. The opening line of the work is among the shortest in the novel:

> Dawn arrived and suddenly from the back door of the house the smell of the lotus tree wafted in so it was hard to breathe and thinking that it was just as if her breath would be strangled by the smell of the flowers Auntie Oryû opened her eyes looked at the photograph of her husband Reisuke floating up in the dim white darkness in a frame set on a stand placed by the side of the Buddhist altar and felt as if having been married to this man Reisuke-san as venerable as the Buddha was an impossible illusion.

Contrast these unfurling lines with the opening sentences of the earliest realist novels, whose crisp and syntactically simple prose, shorn of literary allusion, were appreciated as the hard-earned markers of literary modernity. Two of modern Japanese literature's most famous novels being this way: "They had finished loading the coal" (Mori Ôgai, *The Dancing Girl*, 1890); "I always called him Sensei" (Natsume Sôseki, *Kokoro*, 1914).

Among the progenitors of this kind of Japanese prose style, viewed as the most modern of its time, Kunikida Doppo stands out for answering the demand for a new language of realism that did not incur aesthetic loss. He did so not by insisting like an antiquarian on a new version of classical allusive intertextuality, but by blurring the outlines of his prose to create a vision and mood of "murkiness": evoking things just beyond vision's reach, allowing those things to linger in the distance, uncanny, sublime. This was a method Doppo borrowed from a contemporaneous painting technique that blurred outlines and left much blank space on the canvas, a method undertaken in pieces like his 1897 story, "Old Man Gen," where he recovered a "traditional Japanese" suggestiveness and set it to modern themes and settings.

One writer in particular stands out for having created a literature of enchanted realism by, counterintuitively, stripping prose down to its most basic, parched condition. For writers and critics in the 1930s and beyond, the concrete language of Hitomaro was reborn in the twentieth-century novelist Shiga Naoya, known by many fellow writers and critics in his time and after as the God of Japanese Novelists—much like Hitomaro, revered as a god in his own time. Shiga produced one long prose piece and dozens of short stories. He wrote his masterpiece, *A Dark Night's Passing*, in fits and starts from 1912 to the late 1930s. Not much happens in the novel. Scenes are strung together with little concern for plot and little development in the protagonist, Tokito Kensaku. He looks about him, and we see what he sees in great detail. Sometimes he has emotional reactions to what he sees, and we are given them, too. The prose is simple, the vocabulary strikingly minimal. Things are either "pleasant" or "unpleasant."

The final section of the novel was published in 1937. Kensaku, scarred by his wife's infidelity and longing for peace, leaves on a trip into the countryside. He travels to a Buddhist holy site, seeking peace and perhaps ecstasy, where he has a vision: He "felt as if he had just taken a step on the road to eternity. Death held no threat for him. If this means dying, he thought, I can die without regret. But to him then, this journey to eternity did not seem the same as death."

As a literary experience, the novel is a slow ride. *A Dark Night's Passing* taxes the reader. Why is it considered a pinnacle of modern literary art in Japan? It is about jealousy and dreams of escape, and it describes not much more than one man's perceptions of his concrete world. It masterfully evokes the experience of boredom and convinces the reader that she has before her an artless picture of reality. Shiga is a realist who does not rely on the fancies of the imagination. His novel seems to move according to no structuring principle.

Writers and critics have been drawn to a quality in Shiga they describe as an unadorned bodily naturalness, a prose bodied forth in concrete language undisturbed by thought. For them, Shiga's is poetry of concrete surfaces shorn of evaluation or intellection; his prose possesses a craftsman-like simplicity that calls little attention to itself and all attention to the world. For some critics, Shiga seemed to embody the classical artistry of language, projecting a concrete vision of the world that was a cure for the illness of abstract modern vision. Shiga may have been called the God of Japanese novelists because his prose seemed devoid of literary artifice: he achieved the transparency that many writers sought as the proper vehicle for describing the world as is, a style shorn of classical adornments and intertextual play.



Shiga, like many modern novelists, sought to describe reality as it came to his senses. Since he believed that our lives are mysterious, what he saw on the surface of things allowed him to look beyond it, to an experience of mystery, in the things we do not understand rather than in what we do. He worked to connect the material to the invisible because mystery to him was deepened by contact with concrete reality.

Japanese novelists have spoken of Shiga in tones of anxiety, as a writer to be admired, but not to be imitated. To Kobayashi Hideo, Shiga's most brilliant critic and Japan's first modern literary theorist, Shiga's prose is "as vivid and fresh as the pain of a toothache that pulsates down into the belly." Kobayashi's literary and cultural criticism blended serious reflection on aesthetics, literature, history, and politics with a poet's sensibility. His range of interests was vast: from Buddhist aesthetics to European classical music; from the entire history of Japanese and European literature to sculpture, pottery, and painting; from the politics of literature to the literature of war; from poetics to European and Asian thought.

The analysis of literature as a system of creative works goes back in Japan to the eighth century. The preface to Japan's earliest poetry anthology, the 751 *Fondly Recollected Poems* (Kaifûsô), a collection of poems in Chinese, gives an account of the history of Japanese literature to that moment. In 772 Fujiwara Hamanari wrote a poetic rulebook detailing types of and developments in poetry. He contended that Japanese *uta*, or song, once had end rhymes, which had been lost. What formed these early literary historians' sense of Japanese literary history, what gave them their consciousness of a specific Japanese literary history, was their immersion in Chinese literature and criticism. By 905, at the same time as the completion of the first imperially commissioned anthology, Japan had ceased sending official embassies to China. The chief compiler, Ki no Tsurayuki, asserted parity between the native and the Chinese forms; by the time of the second imperial anthology fifty years later, the compilers were doing philological investigations of the *Man'yôshû*, whose orthography had become difficult for anyone but the scholarly reader. Major works on Japanese poetics appeared over the following centuries, culminating in the eighteenth-century masterworks of philological analysis by the doctor, scholar, philologist, and thinker Motoori Norinaga, whose readings of tenth- and eleventh-century court aesthetics came to dominate how Japanese readers themselves understood what was natively essential about their poetry and aesthetics. Norinaga's notion of the spontaneous emotional response to Japanese poetry informed the thinking of Kobayashi Hideo.

Kobayashi admired in Shiga's prose its spontaneity, its absolute lack of hesitation; "The ripples that spread atop the water are captured before their rippling ends.... It has a sensuousness we can smell and feel. Its sentences build up in a natural flow, in masses. It is formed without composition." Shiga's prose is "like a snake raising its head to the sound of a whistle," and "like the wings of a snow grouse turning to white with the invasion of winter." To Kobayashi, Shiga's aesthetic power is spiritual, creating epiphany upon epiphany, musically. Shiga turns the concrete world into one enchanted, through the force of rhythm. Kobayashi valued a bodily, nonintellectual response to art. Drawing on the writing of Eduard Hanslick, the nineteenth-century German musicologist, Kobayashi hoped to raise literature to the expressive heights of music, leaving content behind and thus becoming able to speak across all generic boundaries. The beauty of the medieval *Tale of Heike* appealed to him because it was the product of a communal audience who listened to it as music—it was a "symphony written in the minor key" by tradition itself. Shiga's aesthetic power was seen as having the quality of music that allows it to create epiphanies and to enchant it through its lingering on the concrete details of this world.

Kobayashi's seemingly gnomic, even cryptic comments on Shiga belong to a literary critical tradition going back in Japan to the eighth century and, before that, to China, in which criticism was itself a poetic undertaking, evaluating and reconstructing meaning and sense, not just through explication and paraphrase, but also by transmitting the flavor of aesthetic sense. Here, for example, is Ki no Tsurayuki in his preface to the *Kokinshû*: "Ariwara no Narihara [named in the Preface as one of the "six immortals of poetry"] has too much feeling, too few words. His poems are like withered flowers, faded but with a lingering fragrance." Here is his evaluation of Ono no Komachi's poetry: "She is full of sentiment but weak. Her poetry is like a noble lady who is suffering from a sickness, but this weakness is natural to a woman's poetry." And on another poet: "Ôtomo no Kuronushi's songs are rustic in form; they are like a mountaineer with a bundle of firewood on his back resting in the shade of the blossoms."

During the decades around the turn of the twentieth century, Japanese writers voraciously reading European and other non-Japanese literatures met a deep and rich native tradition that sparked a wealth of unprecedented literary experimentation unmatched to this day. This is the period that produced Natsume Sôseki, whose work manifestly grows out of his vast reading in the treasures of the Japanese and Chinese literary pasts as well as in the monuments of modern world literature and thought.



In Sôseki's literature, the power of words and their reach beyond language were no longer born of the intertextual ricocheting of words in an echo chamber of tropes, as they had been for his classical predecessors. Rather, the power of his words emerged through a language of realism that refused intertextuality, that was meant to refer not to other words but to the world itself. This was a language meant to be an unadorned, unornamented window onto the world.

Sôseki is known for his message to the modern Japanese middle classes: modernity is a hard and lonely and alienating road. This kind of exhortation was the dominant mode of the time, in tune with the range of hortatory rhetoric directed at people undergoing the upheavals of modernization. It is no small irony, then, that Sôseki used the language he did to write of what words could not capture.

In 1907 Sôseki left his lectureship in English literature at the Imperial University of Tokyo and began regularly serializing novels for the *Asahi News*, a career that ended in 1915 with his death, his final work unfinished. He began his literary venture as a call to arms: "Until now, we have confined ourselves to resuscitating past literature and imitating Western literature. It should be from now on that a true Japanese literature emerges." This literature, he wrote, "will not be a reproduction of or subservient to any other literature, but an expression of a true voice, a voice without shame."

Sôseki answered his own call in his 1914 *Kokoro*, Japan's iconic modernist novel. *Kokoro*, published the same year Mori Ôgai dismissed the modern novel, reveals the traps language sets in the exploration of the human heart. It is about a teacher who purports to transmit wisdom, but the structure of the novel makes that transmission impossible to believe.

*Kokoro* tells a simple story. A young man is attracted to an older man he comes to call his "teacher." He senses a deep darkness in the teacher, who repeatedly drops hints to the boy of the cause of his soul's corruption, never quite revealing anything much at all. Of course, the mystery of the teacher's darkness attracts the boy even more. All that is clear for most of the novel is that the teacher's ailment—his alienation, his loneliness, his ennui, his aggravated self-consciousness—is an urban, modern one.

The action of the novel, narrated by the boy, ends after its first two chapters. At that point the boy has left Tokyo, and his teacher, for the countryside, where the ills of modernity have been kept at bay, to be at his ailing father's side. The third and final section, occupying half of the entire novel, is the teacher's letter—his "testament"—to the boy, in which he describes how his betrayal of his best friend by stealing the object of his love, and then marrying her, had led to that friend's suicide. The teacher, too, the boy learns as he reads, has resolved to kill himself, and we are told in the letter that by the time the boy has received it he has ended his life.

In the final pages of the letter, and of the novel, the teacher writes of the passing of the Emperor Meiji—the symbol of Japan's entry into modernity and the spiritual font for many of Sôseki's generation. Soon, General Nogi (a key figure for Mori Ôgai's thinking about the place of the self in the novel form) commits ritual suicide following his lord, and this event seals the teacher's decision to do the same. The teacher wants to teach:

> Without hesitation, I am about to force you into the shadows of this dark world of ours. But you must not fear. Gaze steadily into the shadows and then take whatever will be of use to you in your own life.... You wished to cut open my heart and see the blood flow. I was then still alive. I did not want to die. That is why I refused you and postponed the granting of your wish to another day. Now, I myself am about to cut open my own heart, and drench your face with blood. And I shall be satisfied if, when my heart stops beating, a new life lodges itself in your breast.

Throughout the novel, we have seen secrets kept and lies told, and we hear from the teacher that whatever he has to say to prevent tragedy taking over other peoples' lives—his wife's, his childhood friends', his young devotee's—is always said too late to have any effect. We see that people seem unable to free themselves from their pasts, and are doomed to repeat them, and we sense that we may be doomed as well to learn precious little from our teachers and parents. This is the lesson of Japan's most ardent literary teacher of the dark side of modernity.

In this, the final third of the novel, the readers are reading the teacher's letter in the hands of the boy as he peruses it on a train returning him to Tokyo. The novel is structured by such triangles. Formally, the novel itself is tripartite, and its central tragedy occurs because of a love triangle: one driven by the teacher's raw, shattering jealousy at the sight of his best friend's passion for the woman who, having thus ignited the teacher's ardor, becomes his own wife. In the final section, though, one may perceive at last a straight line that connects several minds across space and time—a line from Sôseki the writer, through the teacher who has written, through the boy who reads him, and, ultimately, to us, novel in hand, reading with and through them all. There is a merging of more than one consciousness produced through this chain of reading and writing, and even the suggestion of direct communication. And there is also a reminder of the inescapable web of writing and reading that encompasses all acts of literary creation.

The figure of Sôseki as the teacher of modernity's depredations has become iconic, his writing appearing in school curricula, his image on paper currency, his life and lessons kept alive in public memory. Likewise, the lives of Sôseki's characters remain very much alive for all educated Japanese even today. In literature, he stands inimitable, a towering figure whose genius chanced to manifest itself at a time of extraordinary cultural and political transformation. In life, Sôseki was the first and most masterful diagnostician of the travails of modern loneliness, and a moralizing public preacher (who read Emerson) hoping to save souls. His literature, more complex than his speechifying, has been put to many uses.

The most recent queer reading of *Kokoro* can be seen in a play produced in 2008 by a gay theater troupe. An openly gay student is writing his thesis on *Kokoro* and argues that Sensei's suicide was due to his love for his best friend K. Drawing on a dizzying set of influences—Chinese poetry (which Sôseki also wrote), classical Japanese literature, the corpus of European literature and thought (most especially the work of Jane Austen, Samuel Richardson, William James)—in a dozen novels written between 1905 and 1915, Sôseki expanded beyond measure the possibilities of Japanese literary language. With each novel, he experimented anew with generic conventions (including melodrama, detective fiction, realism) and styles (from neoclassical to modern) to arrive at a pellucid prose that plumbs human psychology and emotion in the press of family and social life. And always he wrote with an eye to the human cost of life in the world, while maintaining a sense of the very literariness of man's attempt to render that world. Sôseki became, by the second decade of the twentieth century, a dark modernist, combining in any given novel the prolix writing of Richardson, the irony of Austen, the architecture of the great European nineteenth-century novelists, the psychological insight of William James, or the lacerating emptiness of Conrad, not to mention the melancholy inherited from the classics of his own tradition.

Sôseki was a global writer, not in the expanse of his readership but in the breadth of his own reading and in the contemporaneousness of his work. He was among the final generation of Japanese writers who had been initiated into the world of literature through the Chinese classical tradition. While Sôseki's destiny was to write in Japanese, his literary lineage, his imagination's prism, was global. What made him particularly Japanese, perhaps, was that even when writing about the most pressing matters of his time, he innately understood that literature's most direct attempts at referentiality were inevitably conditioned by a membrane of literature. It was no doubt because of this richly textured literary sensibility that he was able to write, in his 1907 *A Theory of Literature*, what may have been the first global and scientific theory of literature and literary affect—well before either the Russian formalists or I. A. Richards.

Sôseki is concerned with the impression words make on the human sensorium: "One can perhaps approach the form of literary substance with the expression (F+f). F here indicates impressions or ideas at the focal point of consciousness, while f signifies the emotions that attend them. In this case, the formula stated above signifies impressions and ideas in two aspects, that is to say, as a compound of cognitive factor F ('big F'), and the emotional factor f ('small f')."

The question of how to write original literature, to avoid drowning in a tidal wave of influence from both within and without the tradition, and to refresh language and rescue it from cliché, was faced with intelligence, originality, and literary flair by one of modern Japan's most celebrated storytellers, Akutagawa Ryûnosuke, whose work embodied forms of artistic redemption for what he and many of his contemporaries considered a moribund Japanese literature. Akutagawa is one of Japan's iconic artistic figures. His suicide in 1927 marked for some Marxist critics the end of hope in modernity and the start of an abiding sense of crisis and loss.

Akutagawa is a late figure in the longstanding (going back as far as Ki no Tsurayuki in the tenth century) Japanese tradition of striving to achieve the correct naming of things, and of mourning the ancient power of words. In the eyes of Marxist critics committed to the capacity of language to represent life as it is and to transform people and society, Akutagawa was just a petty aesthete.



Not long before his suicide in 1927 Akutagawa wrote "Literary, All Too Literary," a hybrid work of prose and poetry that moves, like Japanese poetry, associatively from topic to topic, developing a case against prevailing literary forms and suggesting the existence of a lineage of prose writers, painters, and philosophers imbued with a spirit of poetry that, he believed, had been sapped from the Japanese language. The literary arts had become "confused," he felt, and words were being "misused." Artists now "produced rather than created." Language had become corrupted by the forces of production in the present, by mass journalism, for example, that cheapened language and effected a break in the transmission of poetic resources from the past.

Only by fanning the faint-but-enduring spark that remained from the past could Japanese literature and its universal poetic spirit be saved: "This is a spirit belonging to our ancestors—not only to

Japan's, but to all ancestors—it is the burning of a flame kindled by geniuses and passed on to geniuses, a flame not yet extinguished, neither in prose nor in criticism." That spirit would be revived by poetic novels formed from lyric fragments. They would be like the paintings of Cézanne—alive more in their color than in their design—because color resembles those lyric moments of beauty devoid of the slightest trace of narrative construction.

Akutagawa imagined a stylistic transformation through which a language of surfaces and "carnal beauty" would triumph over the revelation of meaning and depth. This was to be a musical language, whose "inherent melody" lay dormant in Japanese classical forms, waiting to be awakened, and whose rhythms lived still in older writers—writers like Kôda Rohan—who, decades before, still knew the "echoes of the Japanese language." Akutagawa called for a revival of the rhythmic, musical spirit of words, and hoped for the arrival of a great poet to bring to life "that thing echoing—that green something moving in the poems of Japan's past."

The artistic means that would anchor this new, but old, literary creativity was improvisation, a riffing on past forms. Akutagawa was as intimately familiar with Rodin, Gauguin, Dante, and Ambrose Bierce as he was with the prose and poetry of his own tradition; indeed, he seems even more intimate with his fellow European modernists than with his reclaimed literary forebears, whom he discovered through modern eyes. He was aware that Japanese writers and artists could be dismissed as mere imitators and as "underdeveloped." But his fear that this cultural crisis was irreversible catalysed his attempt to recover, or construct anew, a literature of improvisatory imitation.

To Akutagawa this was to be a new kind of imitation understood as a process of "assimilation." It would move slowly forward by tracing the past, its practitioners understanding that even though there is no such thing as progress in the arts, one must, to continue the work of literature, nevertheless proceed in the illusion of progress. It offered an alternative to the imitation of European forms that had left many writers feeling culturally depleted. Akutagawa contested the distinctively European terms of modernity by revitalizing the classical tradition of improvising on other works of literature. In this way, drunk on literary influence, he embraced imitation—what he called the "art of the ancients"—as the greatest source of creativity.

Calling upon the art of the ancients was one response to an anxiety about cultural borrowing, an anxiety that became a rich source of comic cultural irony, and the very provenance of the literary imagination of the novelist Tanizaki Jun'ichirô, author of such classic works as the 1924 *Naomi* and the 1948 *The Makioka Sisters*, as well as a translation into modern Japanese of *The Tale of Genji*.

Tanizaki wrote erotically playful novels of sexual obsession. In his 1956 novel, *The Key*, an elderly man tries to regain his erotic powers by spying on his daughter and her boyfriend; in his 1929 novel, *Quicksand*, he described cruel sexual games and dangerously domineering women. But in Tanizaki's hands, sexual power could also be a playful, ironic metaphor for cultural relations between Japan and the West. In *Naomi* (literally, *Love of a Fool*), that relationship was inscribed in an ironic take on sadomasochism, in which the masochist (Japan) controlled the sadist (the West) by manipulating the very allure that had been projected on it.

As with Sôseki, Akutagawa, and dozens of other writers before him, Tanizaki's imagination was cast as much by his reading in European as in Japanese letters. When his novels spoke directly to that cultural situation, he did so with confident irony. This is as true in his fiction as it is in his 1934 paean to a lost Japanese aesthetic of shadows, *In Praise of Shadows*:

> I should like to consider the importance of the difference in the color of our skin. From ancient times we have considered white skin more elegant, more beautiful than dark skin, and yet somehow this whiteness of ours differs from that of the white races.... The Japanese complexion, no matter how white, is tinged by a slight cloudiness.... Thus it is that when one of us goes among a group of Westerners it is like a grimy stain on a sheet of white paper. The sight offends even our own eyes and leaves none too pleasant a feeling.

Tanizaki's irony, easily mistaken for yet another sentimental paean to a lost past, here transforms the denigrated darkness of skin into a source of native artistic power, bespeaking the confidence of a writer who has transcended both national and linguistic boundaries of literature.

**3. Nighttime in front of a Japanese restaurant: patterns of light and shadow invite us into the recesses of yet more patterns of light and shadow, where beauty will nurture us in both body and spirit. In his essay "*In Praise of Shadows*," Tanizaki Jun'ichirô elevated the shadows cast in Japanese literature, art, and life to the apogee of Japanese aesthetics.**

Nearly half a century later, in 1968, when he represented himself to the world in his Nobel acceptance speech, Kawabata Yasunari displayed yet another style of ironic self-presentation. A dedicated surrealist writer who only appears to naively embrace an unsullied cultural past, Kawabata drew his inspiration from the Buddhist sphere of Japanese literary aesthetics, the sad, austere, autumnal qualities evoked by the Buddhist medieval poets Myôe and Ikkyû. Their mysterious, suggestive, and inferential poetry belonged squarely within the classical tradition, while its sensuality was akin, in his mind, to European Symbolism. In embracing this aesthetic, Kawabata was also alluding to a tradition shot through with the Indian, Chinese, and Japanese Buddhist distrust in the reliability of language, a tradition in which life-as-dream had become an aesthetic given. At the heart of this literary sensibility were what he calls "eyes at the final moment," which glimpse enlightenment just as they are about to close forever. What can be more ironic than the fact that "eyes before death" came to Kawabata from Akutagawa, who, in his suicide note—a literary piece as famous as many a great novel—wrote that, "nature is beautiful because it comes to my eyes before death."



Kawabata was a surrealist, speaking, as he neared the end of his life (he committed suicide four years after his Nobel Prize acceptance speech), through the language of Buddhism. His gift to world literature was a set of sensual, erotic, strange, dreamlike-but-gritty short stories and novels—at once magical and realistic. Kawabata was a great experimenter with form, a master of the epiphanic prose-poem short story, the fractured narrative of modernity, and the seamless amalgam of European and Japanese literary expression. Kawabata's masterwork *Snow Country,* a short novel he began in 1934 and completed in 1948, tells the story of a bored Tokyo intellectual, Shimamura, seeking honesty and authenticity in the countryside, in the land of snow.

Shimamura feels alienated from the landscape; he has lost the power—the *kotodama*—of language, and the capacity to create

**4. A snow-bound hot spring resort, enclosed by snow-dusted trees, tucked snuggly into a frosted hillside, hard against a cold river sluicing through a narrow valley: an iconic image in Japanese literature and art, and the setting of Kawabata Yasunari's novel *Snow Country*, suggesting frozen emotions and the possibility that they might thaw.**

authentic art. The world of the novel is a canvas painted with the blended palette of sensual experience and literary imagination. The narrative develops according to the pacing of a Nô play, in what is known as the *jo-ha-kyû* rhythm, which is the gradual build-up, the increase in speed and tension—rapid, ecstatic climax—just as its characters also derive from the stock characters of Nô. The protagonist has been lured to the snow country by the memory of a young geisha, Komako, who serves as a blank canvas on which to paint not only the colors but also the sounds, smells, and vibrations of the natural world. Kawabata conjures her through touch and smell: "The dusky green of the cedars seemed to reflect from her neck," and her skin like "white porcelain." The snow country itself, like Komako, is a transparency, a canvas, a template for the senses.

In the final line of Kawabata's novel, Shimamura loses his identity in an oceanic moment that is not only bright but also loud: "As he caught his footing, his head fell back, and the Milky Way flowed down inside him with a roar." Sound, like language, is not merely figurative; it infuses a body with color. It possesses magical power and creates through enunciation, like *kotodama*, the ancient magical power of words. Kawabata beautifully imagines this moment of merging and disruption, of simultaneous communion and alienation: "All of Komako came to him, but it seemed that nothing went out from him to her. He heard in his chest, like snow piling up, the sound of Komako, an echo beating against empty walls. And he knew that he could not go on pampering himself forever."

Kawabata's magic drew from French surrealism and classical Japanese poetry, infused by the dreamy dissolution of the boundaries between reality and illusion taught by Buddhism. In the 1930s, the folklorist, classical scholar, poet, and avant-garde novelist Orikuchi Shinobu heard in Kawabata's novel a sound emanating from the border of death, a poetry that caused "a quiet stirring in the heart."



To Orikuchi, Kawabata was the channel through which the poetry of the ancients and the vibration of the world of the spirit were reborn. The sound of death that Orikuchi heard in Kawabata's novels was the same sound that he wrote into his own work. Orikuchi's 1936 *Testament of the Dead* is set in the eighth century and written in the multiple modern and classical forms of the Japanese language. While the characters speak in the modern language, the narrator always speaks in the classical register, which embodies the sensuality of language. Orikuchi ventured that Japanese literature began with the sensual incantation of ancient songs: As the novel begins, a man awakens into darkness. "A barely audible sound—*shhhh*—followed by something that sounded like punctuation—*ta. Shhta shhta shhta.* What were these quiet sounds that reached his ears? . . . And the sound of dripping, reverberating off the stone—*shhta shhta.* The sound of dripping water?"

# Chapter 4
# Writing violence

The vibration of the world: in the fourteenth century, Buddhist monk and essayist Yoshida Kenkô evoked the realm of the invisible through the world of concrete things. His work was one aesthetic summit of this dominant strain of the tradition. How, then, did writers render the most concrete of experiences, that of violence? Through the centuries Japanese writers have also grappled with bringing literary form to the experience of violence, natural and man-made. Before the twentieth century, this stream of writing reached its apogee in the thirteenth-century *Tale of Heike* and *An Account of My Hut*, and in the eighteenth-century puppet plays of Chikamatsu Monzaemon. In these works, violence is rendered poetically and cast in a melancholy Buddhist light.

In his 1721 masterpiece, *Love Suicides at Amijima*, Chikamatsu, like Sôseki after him, shows us what it means to die for love through suicide. (The play opened just two months after the real-life events on which it is based.) A lovesick merchant and a despondent courtesan become passionately attached. Torn between respect for his marriage and a ravaging passion for one another, the couple kill themselves. Chikamatsu wrote for both actors and puppets, for the Kabuki and the puppet stage. In the puppet plays (bunraku) the tragedy of passion penetrates and harrows the viewer. The text is stylized and musically chanted, and the performance is multi-sensual. The uncanny aliveness of

**5. The magic of bunraku: two puppeteers, draped in black, all but disappearing behind a puppet. The puppet—a woman—stands half their size; she is dressed brightly in red and light blue, a burst of color atop her head; her face is a mask, exhibiting a labile range of emotions as the puppeteers move it subtly, the light playing across its surface.**



the plain-to-be-seen artificially manipulated puppets, and the shadowy puppeteers working them from behind like shadows of destiny, give the play its emotional punch. But the effect grows too from the very musicality of the words.

The play begins with the rhythmic chanting of nonsensical words that have continued to puzzle Japanese scholars. The narration then resumes:

> The love of a prostitute is deep without measure; it is a bottomless sea of affection that cannot be emptied or dried up. By Shell River, love songs in every mood fill the air, and hearts stop short at the barrier of doorway lanterns. Men roam the streets in high spirits, humming snatches of puppet plays, mimicking the actors, or singing bawdy ballads as they pass; others are drawn into the houses by samisens played in upstairs rooms. But here is a visitor

> who hides his face, avoiding the gift day. See how he creeps along, afraid to be forced into spending too much.

A married man and the prostitute with whom he has fallen in love seek to cut their ties to the world and be reborn together but are haunted by their this-worldly duties. They weep and thrash and sob. He prepares to hang himself with her under-sash:

> Its fresh violet color and fragrance will be lost in the winds of impermanence; the crinkled silk long enough to wind twice round her body will bind two worlds, this and the next. He firmly fastens one end to the crosspiece of the sluice, then twists the other into a noose for his neck. He will hang for love of his wife like "the pheasant in the hunting grounds."

And he guides her to stab herself:

> They cling to each other, face pressed to face; their side locks, drenched with tears, freeze in the winds blowing over the fields. Behind them echoes the voice of the Temple.... She smiles. His hands, numbed by the frost, tremble before the pale vision of her face, and his eyes are first to cloud. He is weeping so profusely that he cannot control the blade.

He then thrusts the sword in her.

> Stabbed, she falls backwards, despite his staying hand, and struggles in terrible pain. The point of the blade has missed her windpipe, and these are the final tortures before she can die. He writhes with her in agony, then painfully summons his strength again. He draws her to him, and plunges his dirk to the hilt. He twists the blade in the wound, and her life fades away like an unfinished dream at dawning.... For a few moments he writhes like a gourd swinging in the wind, but gradually the passage of his breath is blocked as the stream is dammed by the sluice gate, where his ties with this life are snapped.

The puppet plays in the style perfected by Chikamatsu began in the early seventeenth century. Blind storytelling minstrels joined forces with popular puppeteers and the twang of the stringed samisen. With the invention of printing, plots and stories could be written and transmitted. Chanters fashioned stories into musical narratives. The music expresses the emotion at any given moment; it can be quick, jolting, or solemnly slow, and the samisen can weep, whimper, wail, laugh, lash out in anger—and frenetically startle. The singing is vibrant and deep. Chikamatsu, the first professional bunraku playwright, often wrote with his chanters, and he wrote for them in mind. The puppeteers too were involved in phrasing and rhythm, gradually increasing tempo to a fast peak and slowing down the cadence as the audience is entangled in heightened pitches of intensity. As in salsa, there is tension and release, tension and release, and if it is successful, the audience participates in the emotions of the drama.

It is the power of rhythm to work on the human sensorium that allows Chikamatsu's work to soundly find its métier in the subject of violence. The combined aesthetic force of his performed plays can be emotionally shattering. This even though his art is decidedly not a mimetic one, as Chikamatsu explains:

> Art is that which occupies the narrow margin between the true and the false.... It participates in the false and yet is not false; it participates in the true and yet is not true; our pleasure is located between the two.... If we represent a living thing exactly as it is, for example, even [the legendary Chinese beauty] Yang Guifei herself, there would be something arousing disgust. For this reason, in any artistic representation, whether the image be drawn or carved in wood, along with the exact resemblance of the shape there will be some deviance, and after all that is why people like it. It is the same with the design for a play....

Chikamatsu's depiction of violence is deeply informed, too, by a Buddhist sensibility: he understands that the suffering that accompanies one's attachment to beautiful things (perhaps perversely) gives rise to a love for them. The Buddhist insight into the suffering that accompanies attachment gave rise to a particular way of loving things of beauty. There are no more famous lines in the Japanese tradition than the opening of the 1212 prose poem by Kamo no Chômei (1153–1216), *An Account of My Hut*—lines that come from a world of pain—for no beautiful thing can last: "The flow of the water is ceaseless and its water is never the same. The bubbles that float in the pools, now vanishing, now forming, are not of long duration: so in the world are man and his dwellings."

The narrator, a monk, has fled the great city of Kyoto and its calamities—fire, earthquake, war, famine. Having witnessed the destruction of all that he deemed beautiful, and all that he cherished for that reason, he built himself a hut and so tried to sever his attachments to the world—only to come to love, and to develop a deep attachment to, the sights and sounds of nature and the beauty of the hut itself. Chômei describes a world that is solidly there but also melting away, being transformed before his very eyes. In this world, one can only achieve a sense of stability through the cultivation of an ironic sense of beauty, a sense that beauty both produces and registers the pain of aesthetic attachment through words not to be trusted as representing truth or security. Beyond the here-and-now are the sounds of the cries of the monkey, the fireflies in the grasses, the sinking of the moon.

The Buddhist truth asserting the pain of attachment is not only manifest in images, but also in sound. Sound hovers also around the great Buddhist aesthetic truth in the celebrated opening lines of the fourteenth-century war tale (the genre goes back to the early eleventh century and blossomed in the thirteenth and fourteenth), *Tale of Heike*, which was chanted by blind minstrels: "The bells of the Gion monastery in India echo with the warning that all things are impermanent. The blossoms of the sâla trees teach us through their hues that what flourishes must fade. The proud do not prevail for long but vanish like a spring night's dream. In time the mighty, too, succumb; all dust before the wind."

For centuries, *Heike* was taken to be verifiable history, real and concrete. It became a treasure house of stories—inspiring war chronicles, *Nô* plays, puppet theater, and twentieth-century bestsellers. Most famously, it describes the downfall of the clan leader Taira no Kiyomori: "Kiyomori's name had been known throughout the land of Japan, and the sight of him would set men trembling. But in the end his body was no more than a puff of smoke ascending in the sky above the capital, and his remains, after tarrying a little while, in time mingled with the sands of the shore where they were buried, dwindling at last into empty dust."

Mishima Yukio, one of Japan's most celebrated modern writers, was enamored with acts of violent loyalty in Japan's military past. Perhaps more than any other Japanese writer, he was keenly attuned to the complex relationship between writing and living violence. In 1949, at the age of twenty-four, he wrote a moving novel of closeted gay anguish, *Confessions of a Mask*. The fantasies of the narrator are graphic and his sufferings intense. It is a short masterpiece about a child's sense of the very strangeness of things, about anguish and isolation in a world destroyed by war. Here is the child narrator's memory as a 12-year-old boy looking at a picture of a renaissance painting of St. Sebastian:



> The black and slightly oblique trunk of the tree of execution was seen against a Titian-like background of gloomy forest and evening sky, somber and distant. A remarkably handsome youth was bound naked to the trunk of the tree.... His white and matchless nudity gleams against a background of dusk. His muscular arms, the arms of a praetorian guard accustomed to bending of bow and wielding of sword, are raised at a graceful angle, and his bound wrists are crossed directly over his head. His face is turned slightly upward

> and his eyes are open wide, gazing with profound tranquility upon the glory of heaven.

The image leads to a bodily reaction:

> That day, the instant I looked upon the picture, my entire being trembled with some pagan joy. My blood soared up; my loins swelled as though in wrath. The monstrous part of me that was at the point of bursting awaited my use of it with unprecedented ardor, upbraiding me for my ignorance, panting indignantly. My hands, completely unconsciously, began a motion they had never been taught. I felt a secret, radiant something rise swift-footed to the attack from inside me. Suddenly it burst forth, bringing with it a binding intoxication....



In this early work, art is the conduit to life, and the self is nothing other than its own performance. Mishima's life came to be as knowingly plotted as his novels, shot through with both desire for wild abandonment and intense discipline. He was intoxicated by the cerebral life of the mind, by literary words, and also by the unthinking life of the body. He famously said that he wanted to shift the center of his consciousness from the one to the other. Beginning in the 1950s he transformed his body into a muscular work of art that he displayed in full camp mode to the public in art photographs and minor roles in B-movies.

In 1970 Mishima transformed, once and for all, his art into life and his life into art in a spectacular performance, captured on the news. He brought his performative life to a performed end through the act of public suicide. He survived, but, with this, he harnessed his aesthetic longings to political theater and, in a gesture that was both kitsch and irrevocably real, he called for an end to democracy and a revival of emperor worship.

Mishima's ritual suicide—he disemboweled himself and was then beheaded by his chosen second after making a speech atop

Japanese military headquarters—was also an extension of his attitude toward words. Like his young gay protagonist, Mishima wanted to move the center of his consciousness from his mind to his muscles; he wanted to create an art that was fully and exclusively of the body. Drunk as he was with the power of words, even as he possessed the urgent desire to leave words behind, it is no surprise that Mishima was attracted to the enchanted embodiments of the Nô Theater (a genre he had reworked in his 1956 *Five Modern Nô Plays*) and to the avant-garde dance form Butoh (*butō*), which required a transfiguration of the human body and an emptying out of the self.

Mishima may have begun practicing for his life's final performance in *Confessions of a Mask*. Four years before he died, he starred in (and co-directed) *Patriotism*, a black-and-white movie with no dialogue, based on his short story of the same name. Mishima plays an army officer who commits ritual suicide in an act of loyalty to his emperor. His wife follows suit, in loyalty to her husband. The couple moves across the stage like Nô actors, as if emptied of all selfhood, revealing on their faces only passion and pain. The scene is gruesome, but there is music; their demise transpires to the plangent and yearning strains of Wagner's *Tristan and Isolde*.

Mishima's sensibility of devotion and worship was anathema to the equally renowned novelist Ôe Kenzaburô. Ôe was as central to the moral and literary map of Japan in the 1960s as Natsume Sôseki was to the first decades of Japanese literary modernity. Ôe was the second of two Japanese Nobel prizewinners, and in his inaugural speech he politely separated himself from the paeans to Japanese literary vagueness made by Kawabata Yasunari, who was the first. Ôe believed that only concrete, precise, and unadorned language could authentically render the suffering of victims.

Ôe was the spokesman for the first generation of Japanese that came to maturity after Japan's defeat in the Pacific War in 1945.

**6. Yukio Mishima as a martyred Saint Sebastian: the scandalous photograph, commonly associated with this most famous twentieth-century Japanese writer, is one among many that he posed for, revealing his baroque taste for self-exposure and self-concealment.**

His straightforward prose style affected a transformation in Japanese letters, and his outspoken ethical concerns made him the central literary spokesman of the antinuclear politics of his postwar generation. What transformed Ôe himself in the early 1960s from a writer of teenage angst to an ethical writer of greater scope was his visit to Hiroshima in the early 1960s. It was there that he witnessed the human toll of the atomic bombing of that city. He was particularly moved by the spectacle of the bomb's "transformation of natural human blood and cells," still evident in the city's inhabitants. For Ôe, only these scarred victims were the rightful agents of the transformation of pain into politics:

> Hiroshima as a whole must exert all its energy to articulate the essential intellectual grounds for abolishing all nuclear weapons in a way that all of the victims' dehumanizing experiences—the misery, the shame and humiliation, the meanness and degradation—may be converted into things of worth so that the human dignity of the A-bomb victims may be restored. All people with keloids and all without keloids must together affirm this effort.



Ôe believed that the experience of Hiroshima could not be represented in words, and this belief is of particular interest when considering Japanese literature's preoccupation with finding a language beyond language. Ôe believed that the Japanese language lacked the vocabulary to speak about suffering; words like "humiliation," "shame," and "dignity"—words that might have seemed apt to post-bombing Hiroshima, for example—were alien to the Japanese language: "The sentence, 'That boy is full of dignity,' for example, does not flow naturally in Japanese syntax. It sounds like a sentence translated from a foreign language." Through Hiroshima, Ôe came to believe that there did exist, however, a "pure language" of suffering, an eloquent language of silence that had long been there, at work in Japanese literature.

It was in his 1964 novel, *A Personal Matter*, that Ôe gave narrative form to his political and literary awakening.

Throughout the novel, the protagonist, Bird—a college professor who vomits in front of his students from an excess of shame (and alcohol)—runs away from the all-too-real responsibilities binding him to his wife and newborn, deformed baby. Chasing through the revved-up streets of postwar Tokyo, getting drunk, seeking out abject sex, fantasizing an escape to Africa, Bird returns at the end of the novel to his responsibilities. Bird has spent his journey through abjection hoping his baby will die—and even considering killing it. Like Ôe himself in Hiroshima, Bird early in the novel is asked to serve as a witness to suffering.

> When Bird opened his eyes the nurse, like someone walking in a mirror, was already on the other side of the glass partition and wheeling the incubator toward him. Bird braced himself, stiffening, and clenched his fists. Then he saw the baby. Its head was no longer in bandages like a wounded Apollinaire. Unlike all of the other infants in the ward, the boy's complexion was as red as boiled shrimp and abnormally lustrous; his faced glistened as if it were covered with scar tissue from a newly healed burn . . . The baby continued to live, and it was oppressing Bird, even beginning to attack him. . . .

He cannot look at the baby; he cannot hear its cries. But on his journey through Tokyo, Bird learns to see and hear the dignity—the authenticity—of the abject. Mostly this happens through sex. He wants to experience shame by raping an old girlfriend, Himiko, from behind, so that he will not see her breasts. He feels shame for not facing his victim and for making her into a boy. The mortification of a woman's body serves the man's agony of self-elaboration. She is his willing partner. He desires "the most malefic sex, rife with ignominy": "Himiko would have to endure considerable pain, probably her body would tear and she would bleed: we both might be smeared in filth!" Later, "without changing the positions of their bodies they drifted smoothly into intercourse." Once they both finally climax, Bird is transformed and now can, finally, hear the authentic sound of his baby's scream: "Abruptly, opening its mouth wide as if to sink its teeth into Bird's fingers, the baby began to cry in a voice too loud to be believed. Waaaaaaaaaagh-uh.... waaaaaaaaaagh-uh.... waaaaaaaaagh-uh....on and on the baby screamed."

We are reminded here of the cry of *zaaa* in Kôda Rohan's musical language. Himiko comments: "You always feel that a baby's cry is full of meaning," and Bird responds, "It's a lucky thing we don't have the ability to understand." Both the baby and the bomb had become images that were very much imbued with the artistic mood of the 1960s, a mood felt and channeled most intensely and artistically as a desire for answers to ultimate questions. What, for example, was the meaning of life in a prosperous middle-class society in recovery from the devastation of the dropping of two atomic bombs, and from the shackles of Japanese authoritarianism?

Closer to the experience of real violence than Ôe were those writers who experienced the devastation of the bomb firsthand and tried to render that experience into words. Writers like Ôta Yôko and Hara Tamiki. Ôta Yôko wrote *City of Corpses*, the *ur*-work of Hiroshima literature, between August and November of 1945, living, as she later wrote, "on a razor's edge between death and life, never knowing from moment to moment when death would drag me over to its side." The piece (one hesitates to designate its genre) begins with a literary lilt: "The days come, the days go, and chaos and nightmare seem to wall me in. Even the full light of clear, perfectly limpid autumn days brings no relief from profound stupefaction and sorrow: I seem to be submerged in the deepest twilight. On all sides people whose condition is no different from mine die every day."

But that lilt quickly collapses before reality. There is no consolation in form or in philosophical musing on the emptiness of things or in the beauty of loss. Instead, there is this:

According to the specialists studying the situation, the "standard symptoms" include the following:

- fever
- loss of energy
- apathy
- loss of hair (as if pulled out, but with the root attached)
- loss of blood (bleeding at the spots on the skin, nosebleeds, bloody phlegm, hemorrhage, bloody vomit, bloody urine)
- inflammation of the mouth (especially inflammation of the gums)
- tonsillitis (especially gangrenous tonsillitis)
- diarrhea (especially with blood in the stool).



It took a good twenty years before a novel mastering the experience of the atomic bomb would emerge. Perhaps the most powerful and literary novel of the bomb is Ibuse Masuji's 1965 *Black Rain*. It is the story of a man, Shigematsu, trying to secure a husband for his orphaned niece Yasuko. She was in Hiroshima when the bomb fell, and her marriage prospects wither because she is rumored to be diseased by the poisonous black rain that fell from the sky after the bomb's blast. The niece's gradual, then dramatic decline in health makes her prospects of marriage grim. That is the present moment of the novel. Her past—the experience of the bombing itself—is told through her uncle's transcription of her diary from that fateful day on August 6, 1945. To marry her off, he hopes to prove that she is healthy. The larger story of the bomb's consequences is told through his own journal of the event and from an array of other diaries and documents, which Ibuse culled from actual diaries and interviews with victims. The novel makes for gripping reading. Ibuse gives us a transparent view of a decimated world:

> At one end of the bridge, a body lay face up with its arms stretched out wide. Its face was black and discolored, yet from time to time it seemed to puff out its cheeks and take a deep breath. Its eyelids

> seemed to be moving too. I stared in disbelief, balancing my bundle on the parapet, I approached the corpse in fear and trembling—to find swarms of maggots tumbling from the mouth and nose and crowding in the eye sockets; it was nothing but their wiggling, that first impression of life and movement.

At the end of the novel, Shigematsu goes to the pond where he has been raising fish, in symbolic and superstitious defiance of Yasuko's demise. They are, indeed, growing, and a flower he planted is also in bloom. But this is not a sentimental book. It concludes with no possibility of something hovering above the here and now: "Shigematsu looked up. If a rainbow appears over those hills now, a miracle will happen," he prophesied to himself. "Let a rainbow appear—not a white one, but one of many hues—and Yasuko will be cured." And then: "So he told himself, with his eyes on the nearby hills, though he knew all the while it could never come true."



Just before this final passage Shigematsu completes the transcription of his journal. Like the boy at the end of Sôseki's *Kokoro*, we have been reading alongside our narrator. Like that boy praying for his Sensei's life, we have been praying that Shigematu's niece will not succumb, even as we feel the doom that time portends.

Ibuse's transcriptions are windows onto reality, yes, but he wisely signals to us that the world out there is available only through words whose power accrues from the fact that they have already been written. Like Ôe's belief that only the scarred can act as agents of transformation, this is the form a literature obsessed with reading and writing takes in the face of disaster. Before that spectacle, there is no hovering light and no music, but there is the power of words. Ibuse raises this question: Was the Japanese tenuous belief in the power of words finally obliterated by the singular event of violence that visited Japan in 1945, the atomic bombings of Hiroshima and Nagasaki? But a generation later, it would seem that the answer to that question was no.

Facing suffering, writers persisted in believing in the efficacy of their craft in language, this time as they worked to render the depredations of environmental damage. In her 1969 *Paradise in the Sea of Sorrow: Our Minamata Disease*, Ishimure Michiko created an ecological aesthetics to confront the suffering of the victims of mercury poisoning. And in 1975 Ariyoshi Sawako, author of popular novels about women's lives and social problems, published her *Cumulative Pollution*, a novel addressing the toxicity of everyday life. Sixteen years later the literary and cultural imagination was again jolted into an outpouring of aesthetic production by the one-day triple disaster of earthquake, tsunami, and nuclear meltdown.

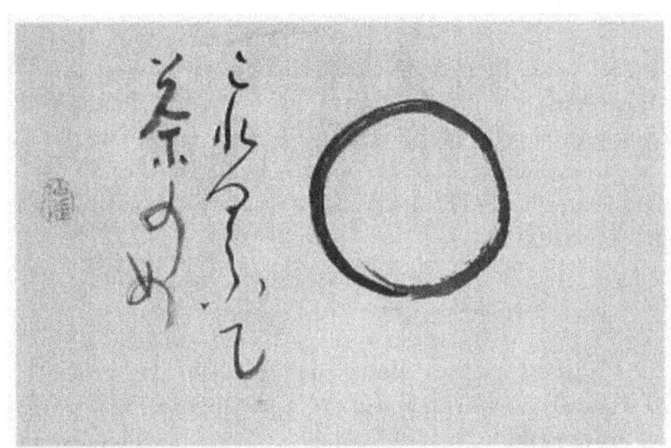

**7. Asked to write a poem just before dying, the Zen monk and poet Shisui drew a circle in ink, an *ensô*: symbol of spiritual enlightenment, the universe, and the emptiness at the heart of all things. In a light and ironic touch, another Zen monk, Sengai Gibon, drew his metaphysical circle alongside the line: "Eat this and have a cup of tea."**

But the tradition also offered the choice of being silent in the face of death. "Death poems" (*jisei*, or "leaving this world") were written by poets deeply informed by Buddhism or who themselves were monks. These verses stretched language beyond itself. In this poem by Hokushi, a seventeenth-century disciple of Bashô, language disappears with the self. The Japanese word for "poppy," *keshi*, also means "erasure."

I write, erase, rewrite
erase again, and then
a poppy blooms.

In 1769, the poet Shisui was dying. His disciples requested that he write a poem. He drew an *ensô*, a circle, a Zen Buddhist symbol of awakening to the non-duality of subject and object, a mark without sound or meaning. At its extreme such a poetics transformed language into image.

# Chapter 5
# The spirit of wordplay

Popular literature spoke of life as it was lived. In Japan, popular literature emerged directly from the practice of storytelling when a popular magazine began publishing straight transcriptions of orally performed tales. When the transcribers responsible for recording these stories went on strike in 1913, writers who were able to create a written style of oral storytelling replaced them. The mid-1920s explosion in readership of mass-circulation newspapers and magazines then turned popular literature into an industry.

One writer in particular makes visible the contours of the popular literary imagination in Japan. Hasegawa Shin wrote in a variety of genres (he was one of those transcribers of oral tales) about violent samurai and suffering lovers, but the genre associated with him, and to which he gave name and fame in 1928, tells of yakuza, wandering gamblers, in search of lost homes and mothers. *Mother Under the Eyelids* was written as a play and novel in 1929, then staged hundreds of times, and filmed repeatedly. Dozens of films are based on Hasegawa's plays, many recapitulating the tales of poor gamblers tending to women in need of saving from illness and poverty.

Hasegawa's yakuza stories have deep roots in both the concrete conditions of local life and the universal stories of the poor.

Hasegawa's gamblers descend from the gambler novels of the 1890s. His are weepy characters whose loyalties are not to a lord, emperor, or state, but to the weak and powerless. In Hasegawa's own words, the yakuza hero is "a man who is unproductive, usually illiterate, wearing a crown of thorns." His heroes serve women gallantly, making them anomalies in popular Japanese narrative. Critics have praised Hasegawa's heroes for their emotional and ethical depth, their devotion not to abstract principles but to concrete, painful situations, and to the discovery of their own selves in those situations.

Such devotion to the concrete as opposed to the abstract is what marks Hasegawa, his heroes, and his vision of popular culture as authentic in the world of popular literature. His lack of education and his direct knowledge of the lives of manual laborers and their codes of loyalty marked him, for critics of popular literature, as authentically popular in his sensibilities and as genuinely linked to an oral tradition belonging to "the people." This is Japanese writing that embraces a transparent and unambiguous relationship among reader, text, and world without the slightest trace of intertextual irony. There were more popular writers like this to come, including Minakami Tsutomu, who blended detective fiction, biography, and memoir in fictions that belonged to both the realms of socialist realism and folktale. He depicted rural poverty in novels such as *The Bamboo Dolls of Echizen* (1963), featuring stock figures of immense appeal like craftsmen, widows, and poor geisha made beautiful by their suffering.



It has been in the popular genres that Japanese literature also displayed its greatest flights of unbridled imagination. In the first decades of the twentieth century, detective fiction sometimes incorporated thinly disguised social critique: promoting the promise of science and rationality and the certainty of progress or indicting the judicial system. Detective fiction in Japan was not weighed down by generic constraints and could be used as a loose envelope for amalgamating ideas about urbanization, sexuality both conventional and perverse, science, ethics, war, and colonialism. In the 1930s, detective fiction engaged the vexing reality of Japanese colonial rule in the South Seas, Korea, Manchuria, and Taiwan. In Oguri Mushitarô's 1933 *The Perfect Crime* (*Kanzen hanzai*), for example, set in a remote part of southern China, the pseudoscience of eugenics leads the detective down a path that ends in the breakdown of reason itself.

Popular fiction brought together streams of thought and culture in brilliantly creative and unexpected ways. In the 1920s and '30s there emerged the capacious imagination of Yumeno Kyûsaku—a pen name that means "eternal pursuit of dream"—onetime Buddhist priest and aficionado of the supernatural subgenres of Nô drama. He also authored supremely original literary works, such as *Bottled Hell* and *The Ends of the Ice* and his most challenging novel, *Dogura Magura*, the precursor of modern Japanese science fiction. *Bottled Hell* narrates a joint suicide by two siblings stranded in the South Seas, who have decided to die together in penance for breaking the incest taboo engendered by their isolation on a deserted island. In *The Ends of the Ice*, suicide is central as well. The protagonist, as soldier, desires to commit suicide with his guide, a "half-Corsican half-gypsy" woman, after having been framed and consequently fleeing the army to Siberia.

*Dogura Magura* combines avant-garde literary moves with a popular Gothic sensibility sifted through the worldview of Freudian psychoanalysis and the sexuality studies of Otto Rank and Richard von Krafft-Ebing. The book begins with the narrator awakening in hospital with amnesia. He has been the subject of an experiment conducted by a now-dead psychiatrist, and the doctors are working to bring back his memories. It is not clear whether he was a psychotic killer or a victim of the strange psychological experiment, but he is told that he killed his mother and wife and that he inherited his psychotic tendencies from an insane ancestor. After the earthquake that destroyed Tokyo in 1923, Yumeno wrote extensive reportage detailing the material and human aftermath of the disaster. In his hands, detective fiction proved to be one of the best literary vehicles for exploring the complex spaces of Tokyo and the anxieties of its residents. Seemingly banal public space was thus exposed as a place of mystery and intrigue.

The greatest writer of detective fiction was Edogawa Ranpo, whose name sounds like Edgar Allen Poe and means Rambling Alongside the Edo River. A reader of Chesterton, Poe, Doyle, Twain, and Dickens (whom he thought to be the fountainhead of the genre) in the 1920s and 1930s, Ranpo wrote a number of masterpieces of entertainment, which afforded his work entry into the canon of "serious literature." These were stories structured around secret codes, fetishes, illicit desires, spectacle, peeping toms, voyeurism, murder, perverse eroticism, dreams and the unconscious, and homosexuality. In his 1928 story "The Beast in the Shadows," a beautiful woman kills her husband and then assumes the roles of three separate characters who set about covering up her crime. Ranpo's 1925 *A Wanderer in the Attic* features a young man with too much money and time; he is a bored urbanite trying to assuage his ennui by crossdressing and seducing men, by spying on the lives of his neighbors from the vantage point of an attic, and, finally, by committing murder.

A wanderer in the city, an anthropologist of daily life, Ranpo was a "modernologist," as the language of the time had it. Modernology, the detailed recording of contemporary daily life, was invented by Kon Wajirô, a designer and sociologist who undertook the detailed description of an urbanizing cityscape and of the habits and gestures of the people living in it. Being a modernologist meant also diagnosing the urban condition. Ranpo's diagnosis was that people in the city suffered from sensual fracture and visual overload; his recommended cure was to shut one's eyes on the world and encase the human sensorium within a cocoon of art: "Other than the art one sees with one's eyes, and the art one hears with one's ears, and the art one analyzes with one's mind, there should also be an art one touches with one's hands." Ranpo was a writer of popular genre fiction in tune with literary tradition as he reached beyond words for an art of the senses.

In the 1960s, mapping Tokyo in words and images provided a radically new way of being in the world. Terayama Shûji's 1969 *Documentary Runaway* was just such a mapping. In its time, it appeared as an avant-garde work with many of the markings of familiar Japanese forms of creativity. It is not, for example, written by a single author, but orchestrated by a master editor. It is the composite work of photographers, poets, essayists, social critics, and young men and women themselves whom the author has encouraged to run away from home toward the city of Tokyo. The book represents their lives in a collage of print media and literary genres and images, including letters, poems, and personal accounts; essays on the theory of leaving home, roundtable discussions among runaways, translation of poems including Allen Ginsberg's long poem *Kaddish*, half-page chapbooks of runaways' verse, folding books of photographs, questionnaires and census reports, song lyrics, maps of Tokyo streets and transportation.

In the 1980s, the conceptual artist Akasegawa Genpei created another kind of community by assembling into a book of photographs submitted by his students and readers to a column he had been writing in a photography magazine. The photographs were of "hyper-art" objects—once-functional objects left behind by urbanization—that he dubbed "Thomassons," after the history of failed bunts by an American pinch-hitter playing for a Japanese baseball team whose bat never connected with a ball. In the book, the pictures were accompanied by Akasegawa's ironic, comic, nihilistic, and nostalgic words about an urban imprint in the process of erasure.

Popular fiction, and especially the detective genre, had its more avant-garde practitioners, including Abe Kôbô, whose 1962 meditation on identity and alienation, *The Woman in the Dunes*, features the case of an amateur ornithologist from Tokyo lost in a sea of sand dunes—where he has, we learn, come to accept his life as a member of a small community of dune dwellers whose sole work is to keep the sand from suffocating them. The novel begins: "One day in August a man disappeared. He had simply set out for the seashore on a holiday, scarcely half a day away by train, and nothing more was ever heard of him. Investigation by the police and inquiries in the newspapers had proved fruitless."

A Japanese (and also a modernist) meditation on real-life matters, *The Woman in the Dunes* signals that whatever happened to its male protagonist is lost in a sea of words. The narrative of the man's adventure proper begins once we are told that though we know he has disappeared, we know nothing else; and the novel concludes with two official documents: a "notification of missing persons" and a "judgment" that officially proclaims the man to have disappeared, though his very existence and death remain unascertainable. Abe Kôbô was to frame many of his existential speculative fictions this way.



These literary anthropologists of urban life wrote in the wake of Japan's greatest modernologist of them all, Nagai Kafû. Kafû's writings about Tokyo continue to be consulted as guidebooks for the city, even as they are strong statements of the inseparability of the real from the literary. Kafû's 1937 *Strange Tales from East of the River* is a modernist antiquarian meta-detective novel. A reader of Zola, Flaubert, and Gide, of the Japanese classics, modern and ancient, of French and Japanese demimonde fiction, and of Chinese poetry, Kafû was famous as a melancholy figure of nostalgia, hiding away in the modern haunts of the demimonde in order to recapture the faded worlds of the eighteenth-century pleasure quarters and the popular writers of that world. In his novels he described worlds in which behavior and language were so immersed in poetic tropes that reality could never fully appear from behind the prism of art.

The plot of *Strange Tales from East of the River* is simple. A writer wanders around the pleasure quarters, meets a young prostitute, visits her repeatedly, and ends the affair. The novel reads like an essay about the moods of a man writing a novel. The language of the work is that of literature itself: it is made up of quotations from the classic Chinese novel *Story of the Stone*, fictitious letters, and various other fictions of the demimonde; and it is shot through with self-conscious literariness. We are trained by the text to remain aware that we are always reading nothing more than a fiction and that we must never believe in the transparency of modern writing. Kafû had no truck with the dominant high-brow literary genre of the time, the autobiographical "I-novel," thought to sincerely express the truth of a writer's life and soul. At the center of the novel we are given another novel written by the narrator. We are also given an alternative ending. Kafû's demimonde, in other words, is a fictional construction, drawn by Kafû from his reading not only of Japanese but also of French literature.

In concluding the novel, the narrator tells us he has met his main character:

> I must now lay down my brush, my strange tale from east of the river finished. To give it an ending in the old style, I should perhaps add a chapter describing how, quite by accident, six months or a year later, I met O-yuki in a wholly unexpected place. She had changed her profession. And if I wished to make the scene yet more effective, I could have the two of us see each other from the windows of passing automobiles or trains, unable to speak, however intense the longing. My scene would have a very special power if we were to pass on ferries, on, say, the murmuring River Tone, in the time of autumn leaves and flowers.

Against a wave of modern realism that threatened to blanch out the beauties of language Kafû held up a mesh of literariness. This was his form of enchantment. For Kafû the material city was enchanted through the gauze of writing.

Kafû wrote in a long tradition of demimonde writing, where women embodied desire and linked the profane and sacred worlds. They were goddesses and shamans, metaphors for life's depredations, guides to moments of ecstasy in sex and in death, binding men through attachment and providing the chance to end all attachments. The demimonde produced philosophical reflection as well. In the 1920s, Kuki Shûzô, a Japanese student of Heidegger, found the cure to the ills of modernity—he thought that modern Japanese were living in a fallen world, a world where human senses, once freshly open to the world, were now deadened—in the aesthetics of the eighteenth-century demimonde. This to him was a world where the senses were integrated and the body whole, and where the body's sensual apparatus corresponded perfectly to the art it produced. What Kuki called *iki* was a sensibility that is plucky and flirtatious, that finds pleasure in playing with but never fully satisfying one's desires, that prevents one from becoming attached to things even as it draws one to them.

It is certainly no coincidence that in the hands of women demimonde fiction revealed a less romantic, less enchanted side of the sexual and entertainment trades. In the 1880s, Higuchi Ichiyô, the first great modern woman writer (who unfortunately died at age twenty-four), chronicled poverty and emotional suffering in the shadows of the demimonde, tapping the genius of a language of finely etched realism, attentive to the grit of life, *Genji*-esque prose (Ichiyô was to some a Murasaki incarnate) that flowed fluidly in and out of her characters' minds, drifting from descriptive passage to indirect speech to quoted dialogue, sinuous sentences taking up in their train narrative asides, poetic punning, allusion, and other literary techniques. Ichiyô's writing was in her time and to the present an object of worship. In 1896 Masaoka Shiki praised Ichiyô's 1895 story, *Child's Play* (in poetic and gnomic terms): "It is a single flower, plucked from something like a heap of filth, which, when it scatters its pure fragrance in the southerly wind, inebriates people with its fragrance."

**8. Higuchi Ichiyô, looking very young but precociously observant, discerning, and world-wise. The patina of this faded image of the writer reflects the hold she has had over countess Japanese readers and writers.**

Directly descending from Ichiyô's lineage was Kôda Aya, Kôda Rohan's daughter and perhaps the greatest writer of demimonde fiction, a brilliant prose stylist whose 1956 novel *Flowing* displays the reality of women's lives through the prism of art. *Flowing* casts a disenchanting shadow over the postwar demimonde but sustains the enchanting quality of feminine artistry. Written in the 1950s, Aya's prose seemed old-fashioned, relying on antiquated words, ellipses of grammatical particles and personal pronouns, sentences ending in nouns (reminiscent of the seventeenth-century novelist of the demimonde, Ihara Saikaku), out-of-use Chinese characters, the melding of dialogue and narrative in single, paragraph-long sentences, and, finally, onomatopoetic language. It is often difficult to determine who is speaking, and about whom. All this reveals her greater interest in euphony over clarity.

These traits have also made Aya an heir to Japanese women's writing stretching back to *Genji* in the eleventh century. It is no exaggeration to say that for all later generations the font of the prose tradition was the literature of the court women of the tenth and eleventh centuries. Bowing to this reality, as early as 935, Ki no Tsurayuki wrote the classic *Tosa Diary* in the voice of a woman. The modern lineage of extraordinary women writers includes far too many to name. Okamoto Kanoko, in works like her 1937 *A Riot of Goldfish*, created a world in which not much happens but which pulsates with an atmosphere of frustrated striving for aesthetic perfection; or a number of 1960s and 1970s writers exquisitely and acutely attuned to states of melancholy and subversive consciousness: Takahashi Takako, who, through a gothic aesthetic informed by ETA Hoffman and Poe, dwelled on the sinister beauty and hallucinatory explorations of women's secret subversive proclivities; Kurahashi Yumiko, Oba Minako, and Yamamoto Michiko, who wrote in anti-realistic idioms of dangerous feminine eroticism; Ogawa Yôko, who wrote of women's murderous desires and jealousies and limned images of female loneliness and madness leading to violence and murder; or

Tsushima Yûko, who in novels like her 1979 *Territory of Light* revealed the workings of a women's aching and dreamy consciousness as it suffused her life of daily struggle.

Mishima Yukio bemoaned the feminine tradition and imputed to Kôda Aya the primary culpability for keeping it alive. He critiqued her style for lacking precisely what Bashô and Shiga were praised for possessing: concreteness. Onomatopoeia was for Mishima the product of mere intuition; it was a fallen language of transcribed impressions. It lacked vigor and the safe distance between writer and reader provided by rigorous, intellectual abstraction. Aya's prose made him feel, in his own words, like he was touching her skin.

The world Aya describes is gritty and very real: the geishas belonging to the establishment that her heroine, Rika, has joined as a maid live hard economic and emotional lives, described in unflinching detail. To Rika, the protagonist of her most famous novel, the 1956 *Flowing*, this world is enchanted by elaborate rituals of coiffure and seduction, by complex systems of performance, and by the ethereal sounds of musical instruments being plucked by geisha. In the following passage, she witnesses a quotidian human gesture that is a work of art:

> Still on her side, she first reaches out her thin hand and flips each layer of the *yûzen* blanket off her. Then, gently raising her upper body with her other hand, her lap crumpling, she shifts into a sideways, seated position. She rises smoothly, as if extracting her body from inside the futon, leaving behind not even the wrinkles of her sleep. Within this woman, dressed in deep purple, deeper than crimson, Rika sees all that could burn, even with an almost spent passion. Perhaps there is nothing left but the memory of a burning past, yet even now she arises from sleep with such elegance. If it is indeed the remains of an art deeply imbued over the long years and no longer capable of being extracted—rather than an eroticism merely gushing up from inside her—this technique of a lifetime is a beautiful thing.

A keen observer of lives lived through performance, Aya taps a spring of Japanese creativity fed by the world of the demimonde, a real and (for Japanese writers) literary place from which emerged a tradition of playful and comic writing—writing that rendered the quotidian reality of a world through the most playful, comic, literary language. (In 1932, the writer Sakaguchi Ango, a reader of the French philosopher Henri Bergson, wrote that farce is "the highest form of art.") At the founding moments of Japanese literary history this kind of performative textual creativity had been unleashed by the collision between spoken Japanese and written Chinese, a collision that reverberated for centuries. A love of wordplay was born of necessity from Japanese's spare phonological system, replete with homonyms and near homonyms. Through the centuries, poetic devices allowed for a play with sounds, meanings, and grammar.

The word *gesaku*—"playful writing"—captures one legacy of this love of wordplay. It was the spirit of playful writing (on which more, in a bit) that in the 1970s fed the creation of the massive, grand, tour-de-force, onomatopoetically named comic masterpiece, *The People of Kirikiri* (1973–81), by Inoue Hisashi. For Inoue, the work of the novelist was to breathe playful life into language. His novel is written in standard Japanese but its Chinese characters are, according to eighth-century practice, accompanied by pronunciation glosses in the (fictional) *Kirikiri* dialect. One character translates canonical works of Japanese literature into *Kirikiri*-ese, selections of which appear in the novel. Even Kawabata's *Snow Country* is subject to local comic reinvention.

For Inoue, Japanese literature had been dominated by a strain of dull prose churning out abstract ideas: a literature bereft of all rhythm and sound, and a music that has forgotten its musicality. As one of Inoue's characters states: "Some writers just keep paring away and paring away superfluous words, then they pare away some more: The Shiga Naoya type. Well, I am paring away and paring away superfluous ideas and then I pare away some more, in just the same way—understand?" Paring down until it becomes pure sound: *kirikiri.*

Inoue's novel is almost just a pretext for wordplay and parody. Sound, once again, triumphs over sense, but in a different way than we have seen before. "Punning," says Inoue, "is the destiny of the Japanese language." When a utopia is established in the fictional land of Kirikiri, non-punning immigrants are not allowed in. Japanese possesses a limited number of phonemes and limited ways of combining them, as well as a large stock of homonyms and near homonyms. Why not—like the classical court poets—tap into the genius of this "limited" language? Inoue writes: "My frequent use of various forms of wordplay could be described as tapping the demonic power of words in order to gain for them greater authority than the actual things they are supposed to signify."



The spirit of wordplay was not at all new: it lay at the heart of the fifteenth-century practice of linked verse, or *renga*. *Renga* sequences were produced in communal poetry sessions of warrior elites, clerics, and amateurs. As few as two and as many as thirty poets might attend. The sessions were ritualized events, practiced alongside other arts such as flower arranging and incense judging. They were dialogic and open-ended, each poet competing to have his or her poem recorded by a scribe. What has been passed down to us are only the written traces of the oral performances judged in their time to have been the best. Many of these sessions were subsequently read, copied, and commented upon by later generations, such that thousands of pages of verses and commentary are extant today. Highly valued in the tradition, they have been anthologized, and much of the scholarly examination of both the theory and practice of the form has itself found a place in the canon.

The sessions during which the *renga* were recited resembled the performances of a small orchestra. The scribe would recite the spoken verse for the next poet, confirming that the link in the chain of poems had abided by the elaborate rules of diction, imagery, and sense governing linkage. Then, with the nodded assent of the *renga* master, the scribe would commit the poem to a particular color of paper, which had been carefully chosen to accord with the season. The scribe watched over the proper adherence to rules while the Master paced the session, orchestrating the artistic development and poetic patterning of the sequence to maintain an overall consistency of tone. Part of that orchestration involved a pattern of rhythm, drawn from court music, of gradual buildup and intensification. Like musicians, the poets improvised on a set sequence of notes: an opening verse, for example, must reflect the season and locale, and draw its diction from the finite, specific poetic lexicon. One fourteenth-century treatise lays out these rules:

> The scribe first kneels by his round mat, and then, at a sign from the person of highest rank, seats himself. Next he removes the lid of the box containing the inkstone, folds the paper, places it on the writing table, and rubs the ink stick on the inkstone.... The ink stick should not be rubbed too long. He then takes up a brush, examines it, then dips it in the ink and lays it with the handle on the brush rest. Next he writes the character for "title," and drawing up his left knee [in a posture of respect] he looks in the direction of the host and awaits the *hokku* [opening verse]. When the *hokku* is given, from whatever quarter, he accepts it, and after conferring with the master at the session, he writes down the rest of the title of the sequence. He then recites the *hokku* and writes it down, then chants it, after which he inscribes the name of the person who composed it. At the pleasure of the host or senior member, he may therefore sit at his ease. After writing the title he may prepare as much ink as he wishes. The leftover folded paper should be placed on the lid of the inkstone box.

In the *renga* performance, meaning served musical wordplay, its palette, rather than the other way around. Here is the *renga* poet extraordinaire, the fifteenth-century monk Shinkei: "The tone of voice with which you recite the offered verses is the most critical aspect of the session.... You must concentrate so that your voice reaches everyone, even in the back. Depending upon the quality of the voice, even a fine verse can sound flat and unpleasant."

This was a world of words that, when inhabited by the most skilled practitioners, could extend mere language into the realm of enchantment. A *renga* handbook might recommend entering a meditative state in order to incorporate into one's body past examples of Chinese and Japanese verse. With his body and mind so absorbed in, and by, words, the poet could tap into their inherent magic. For (and here we see a glimmer of Japan's encounter with the Sanskrit tradition), *renga* was a *dharani*: a mantra, a talismanic utterance imbued with magic.



For Inoue Hisashi, the fiendish power of playful words was only accessible in the hinterlands, in a place like Kirikiri, far away from Tokyo, the center of normative life and language. For Inoue, the lodestar for a new language—one sparse in ideas but rich in language—was the playful spirit of the popular fiction of the eighteenth century that flourished in the days before the advent of the astringent realism of modern literature at the end of the nineteenth and the start of the twentieth century. Inoue fancied himself a latter-day practitioner of this literature drunk with language whose guiding aesthetic was the pastiche.

*Gesaku* does not in itself constitute an identifiable genre. Rather, it is a general rubric that refers to a variety of genres, manifest in thousands of texts, which first emerged in the late eighteenth century. Their unifying spirit has been described as a playful probing of the truth and exposure of art's artfulness. Formally, it can be identified by its concertedly eclectic mixture of styles: classical Chinese expressions read as colloquial Japanese, stiff honorifics interspersed among vulgar terms, Chinese poetry alternating with local slang. In the eighteenth century, *gesaku* exploded in the literate urban capital of Edo (later called Tokyo). Derided later by the self-regarding creators of what they thought to be a sophisticated, modern literature, seen by many literary historians as a frivolous interlude between the detailed realism of Ihara Saikaku in the seventeenth century and the birth of the modern novel in the late nineteenth, *gesaku* recorded the world of the licensed pleasure quarters, in a language steeped in its argot and preoccupied with the connoisseurship of art and desire. For these writers, art was a game that could ironically pierce the vanities and that intertwined the complexities of sexual and economic life.

*Gesaku*'s music of words also had its less refined practitioners. In the eighteenth century, Karai Senryû collected 10,000 verses of comic verse composed at parties by literati. Free of the rules that applied to conventional poetry, they came to be known by the poet's name, *senryû*. A subset of this light genre that broke not only poetic but other proprieties as well was called "propriety-breaking verses." *The Safflower Princess* (naming a chapter from *The Tale of Genji*) was one such work, first anthologized in 1776, contains this exemplary line: "to show his commitment the high priest licks the boy's asshole."

Other types of erotica exuberantly mixed high and low while reveling in the vibrancy of words. Over time, erotic parodies emerged as a counter-discourse to popular Confucian ethics texts. Some dealt with the physical and mental health of women. Some were parodies of children's books. There were erotic versions of serious Confucian ethical tracts such as *The Treasure Chest of Great Learning for Women*, the parody of which—*Great Pleasures for Women and Their Treasure Boxes*—was published in the 1750s. Yet, even in such erotic works it was still the play of language that was of greatest interest to one writer: "There are ten terms for the types of vulvas, ranked as follows. First is the *take* (high); second, *man* (rice cake); third, *hamaguri* (clam); fourth, *tako* (octopus); fifth, *kaminari* (purse); eight, *hiro* (wide); ninth, *shita* (downward); tenth, *kusai* (smelly). . . . The penis has ten names ranked as follows: First, *fu* (soft gluten bread); second, *kari* (sharp head rim); third, *sori* (turns up); fourth, *kasa* (umbrella); fifth, *shakudô* (copper/gold alloy); sixth, *shiro* (white); seventh, *ki* (tree); eighth, *futo buto* (fat); ninth, *naga* (long); tenth, *subo* (covered head)."

In keeping with its eclectic nature, such playful literature often combined narrative and non-narrative passages. The narrative development of a story could pause for a disquisition on Chinese medicine while the writing changed from the easy phonetic script often used for fiction to the harder Chinese for the essay. This kind of pastiche was codified by the term *mitate*, used in reference to painting as well as literature. The term encompasses allusion, parody, and admixtures of classical and modern, sublime and mundane registers. Many of these books drew on a broader world of nonfictional writing: etiquette guides for pleasure seekers, guidebooks to the pleasure quarters, and sermon collections.



Much of this playful writing was a multimedia art. Whereas a modern novel up until the late nineteenth century would typically rely strictly on language to convey meaning, writing like this could seamlessly incorporate the tactile and visual as well. This was not unprecedented. At court, for example, from the eleventh through the fourteenth centuries, poetry and prose might be written alongside paintings on screens, or on dyed and scented paper, in calligraphy that carried its own aesthetic burden. Calligraphy—built upon the Chinese tradition but adapted and transformed in Japan over the centuries—carries the meanings of words but pushes them toward becoming ornaments. Straddling the art of signifying language and the art of abstract design, calligraphy also blurs the boundaries between the spatial and the linear. It expresses personality through shape: through balance, harmony, rhythm, hesitation, thickness, boldness, and fragility.

Until the late nineteenth century, in fact, the close relationship between visual art and literature, between text and image, was not just a given; it can be said to have structured all cultural production. (The modern novel's push for generic purity represented a fierce rejection of this.) Literature flourished as an ensemble of words and pictures, each echoing or enmeshing the other. Literary allusions could be supplied by the details of a picture. Book art and poetry were in this sense indistinguishable, blurring the experiential divisions between picturing and writing, between reading and seeing. At its most extreme, writing itself could be scattered across a page into an abstract design. Such a work as *The Tale of Genji*—to us a novel of the most literary order—was in its time also a visual art, read on dyed papers, sometimes even flecked with gold or silver, its words written in calligraphy that looked like trails of ink running over subtle color palettes.

This fluid practice of combining text with image continued in full force until it hit the gale winds of a modernizing quest for generic purity in the 1880s. Until then, illustrated fiction had dominated the practice of fiction. Many novels showed detailed images on every page. Words and pictures worked in tandem to create narratives. Images could satirize serious text, carrying the descriptive burden, leaving the text to dwell only on dialogue, or picture expressions of emotion that could not be described. Illustrators could anchor and clarify narratives that were written in poetically dense language many readers could not fully fathom without the technological prosthesis of the image.

In the eighteenth century, in Santô Kyôden, we witness a writer who was also famous as an illustrator, producing under a different name, in whose work the world described seems no more than a vehicle for mingling the literary and the visual. Kyôden wrote hundreds of popular works that, although light in import, still required extensive and deep knowledge of a range of genres and media, both visual and verbal, classical and popular literary allusions, as well as the quotidian and complex codes of life in the demimonde. Characters and lines from the Kabuki stage were incorporated and parodied, as were elements of the Nô theater. Pictures and texts interact and contradict one another. Kyôden's *Battle of the Books* is replete with verbal and visual puns about publishing, paper, and writers of the time—everything that goes into making a literary book.

One brilliant example of this visual-verbal imagination is Takizawa Bakin's version of *Chûshingura*, or *The Forty-Seven Loyal Ronin*, one of Japan's most storied historical narratives. It is a story of virtuous retainers committing suicide out of loyalty to their lord. The text is a rebus, a series of drawings of objects representing words or syllables. It calls attention to both the visual and, because the symbols have to be sounded out to make meaning, the aural quality of words.

That Bakin was a major prose stylist says much about the hybrid nature of the literary culture of his time. He was the most important writer of long fiction in the years before a flood of translated works instigated new formal experiments and talk of literary modernity. Bakin's highbrow fiction drew from the Chinese and Japanese classics and was produced through the combined efforts of the great illustrators, calligraphers, and printers of the day. His *Chronicle of Eight Dogs of the Satomi Clan*, the epic account of eight dog-knights with superhuman powers, came out in installments between 1814 and 1842. Written in complex elocutions with many obscure Chinese characters and arcane cultural references, it was a rarefied work. It was also a perfect example of an open-source work, freely recycling literary material from the fourteenth-century Chinese classic action-adventure novel *Water Margin*. The work only achieved its immense popularity later, when it was rewritten by another writer using simplified diction, excising most of the Chinese characters, pruning literary references, and expanding the number of

**9.** The late-eighteenth-century master of the *kibyôshi* genre, Santo Kyôden—writer and illustrator both—tells stories having text and image work in concert. In this image, a high-prestige prostitute is served by her attendant. By their side, a child reads a picture book, much like the one in which he himself is presented to the viewer and reader.

illustrations—all the while sticking close to Bakin's tale, down to the level of sentence structure.

What did it mean, then, to read Bakin? After all, during his time, literature could be—and often was—written in Chinese, and in the various orthographies of Japanese, with phonetic logographs printed alongside each Chinese character. As for the broader literary landscape in which the writers of the time were working, it included the Japanese classics, the sacred texts of Buddhism, theater libretti, local myths and legends, and historical and Chinese philosophical thought. And each of these genres could look different on the page, depending on the art of bookmaking. Associations among images could be created visually through the use of the Chinese ideographs, while the phonetic glosses did the work of conveying the content of the story. Often, the proportion of pictures to text, for example, would determine whether the readers were seeing more than reading or reading more than seeing.



This dynamic was lost in the modern move toward realism, and the crusaders for that new style stripped away the seeing part of reading, leaving only content behind. Visual aesthetics would no longer serve—just as they had ceased to serve when Prince Genji left the scene. Still, some of the words that comprise the verbal component of *Eight Dogs* would, in decades to come, be memorized and recited, and the rhythmic, musical qualities of Bakin's prose would survive, and even thrive, in the transition to realism.

# Chapter 6
# What is Japanese literature?

The spirit of words: this history of Japanese literature concludes by returning to its birthright and deepest wellspring the almost magically unifying, enchanting, and sometimes healing, power of words in the face of what it means to be human.

Beginning in the 1880s, Japanese writers and thinkers participated in a global conversation about aesthetics. In the late nineteenth and early twentieth centuries, the aesthetic thinker Shimamura Hôgetsu ventured to describe the mood of sympathetic immersion of the self in its object of contemplation. The aesthetic moment, Shimamura wrote, occurs when we lose our will as we merge with the object of our concentration. Drawing as much from Edmund Burke as from the eleventh-century aesthetic ideal of *mono no aware*, the sympathetic response to transience, Shimamura argued that such a merging depends on a capacity for sorrow. In a similar vein, the late nineteenth-century Romantic poet and essayist Kitamura Tôkoku, an avid reader of Coleridge, Byron, Carlyle, and Emerson, teased out a notion of the sublime as a place of the "absolute thing," where the self is "annihilated" and we can sense, beyond our capacity to see, the "great, great world of emptiness" bathed by the light of the moon. In the 1930s, the philosopher Ônishi Yoshinori argued that *mono no aware*, which he described as a "dipping into a kind of continuous grief," was an intuition that allowed for a penetration into the essence of being. He also found a kinship between the quality of *yûgen* (mystery and depth), present as far back as the eighth century, and the European notion of the sublime, in a poem like this one from the *Man'yôshû*:

On the vast ocean
not a single island in sight
and yet, far beyond
the rolling surface of the sea,
white clouds rising high.

It was perhaps not a surprise that, bolstered by the growing interest in the Romantic sublime, the *yûgen* of Japanese poetry found a receptive audience among aesthetically minded thinkers in the twentieth century. But it also touched the minds and hearts of Japanese citizens anew during the war years of the 1930s and 1940s. The dominant military song of Japan's years of war and imperial authoritarianism was the lament, "Across the Seas." It was commissioned by the government in 1938 but based on an eighth-century poem by Ôtomo no Yakamochi, the final great poet and editor of the *Man'yôshû*. The song was broadly disseminated through radio and was used in mass youth events, navy broadcasts, government ceremonies, and public reports of Japanese battles:

across the sea, corpses soaking in the water,
across the mountains, corpses heaped upon the grass,
we shall die by the side of our lord.
We shall not die in peace at home.

The pentatonic waxing and waning of the song—with its *kotodama*, its power to enchant, heal, and console—inspired a community of citizens to cohere as loyal subjects bound by blood in war. And this same magical power echoed as well in the melancholy notes of "Our Lord's Reign," Japan's national anthem, composed in the 1930s at the request of the Naval Ministry, adopted for ceremonial purposes by the Imperial Household

Ministry, and made mandatory in primary-school education. The song's lyrics were borrowed from an anonymous tenth-century poem collected by the father of Japanese lyric poetry, Ki no Tsurayuki, whose preface to the *Kokinshû* became the classic statement of the notion that poetry is the spontaneous lyric expression of the human heart.

> May the Emperor's reign last
> for one, for eight thousand generations
> until the small pebbles
> become great rocks
> covered with moss

American officers who heard the song after the war were taken aback by its melancholy—not an emotion they would readily associate with a national anthem. But they were likely unaware that it was the echo of familiar poetry carried along by the somber waxing and waning tones of the music that keyed remembrance and focused attention.



In 905 Ki no Tsurayuki had called for Japanese poetry to "smooth the relations of men and women and calm the hearts of fierce warriors." In the fifteenth century, the poet Shinkei described poetry's effect on the world:

> The mind and language of poetry are rooted in a sense of mutability and sorrow for the human condition. It is through poetry that people convey to one another their emotion about things that have moved them deeply; its influence should soften even the hearts of barbarous demons and stern warriors, leading them to a realization of the truth about this transient world.

Japanese literature heals by enchanting through words, and we can see it doing just that in the 1990s. Kurita Yuki is one writer for whom literature possesses a gentle, ambient quality that would salve the psychic wounds of agitated readers. In Kurita's fiction, the writing positively soothes as in moments like this from the 2005 novel *Hotel Mole*: "The back of the chair was tall, with armrests. The chair was nice.... Even through my clothes, I could feel the suppleness of the leather on my skin. I closed my eyes and soon felt my body yielding to the softness. A moan of comfort began to bubble up from deep within my throat." One critic has said this of this work: "Several times while reading this mysterious story, I was overcome with sleepiness. This certainly was not because I was bored.... In the same way that a delicious description of food triggers hunger, the qualities of sleep were so powerfully portrayed here that I became quite sleepy."

Novels like this make no demands on the reader. They are simply written, and they are attentive to the things that occupy our everyday lives, from which we become more and more divorced as we spend more of our time looking at words and images on a screen. They never refer to other literatures; writers can no longer assume a font of references. They are not, like the tradition behind them, allusive, referring to other literatures and demanding of readers that they have read much, nor are they decorative. But like the works in that tradition, these novels surround the concrete with a vague sense of drifting through a mystery—though that mystery is also comfortable and never demanding. We sense the concrete and the ephemeral in novels like these—we sense the voice of Sei Shônagon. But in the 1990s this voice played more like a fugue away from reality rather than an embrace of it. This is what happens to delicate concrete observation when practiced in an infinitely complex and overwhelming (and technologically obsessed) time—instigating a hasty retreat from the digital back into the analogic experience.



Such a hasty retreat might describe the experience of the protagonist of the best novel by Japan's most translated writer, Murakami Haruki. In the 1982 *The Wild Sheep Chase*, he wanders in a mild state of melancholy through a quotidian world touched by mysterious glimmerings in search of a mysterious sheep with a star on its back. “Mediocrity walks a long, hard path,” one mysterious character intones. It is this quality of resignation to the ineluctable passing of magic in all its forms that makes the fiction of this global writer so familiar to readers of the Japanese tradition. The muted sadness of this young man seems impermeable to the magic that promises to transform his life. At the heart of the novel is the Sheep Man, who comes from a place where time has stopped and words have been destabilized (“Names change all the time”) into the rhythms of music. It is the power of the sounds of words (the *kotodama*) and the music that lies beyond language that beckons him away from the harsh reality of existence—heartbreak, politics, and war—and makes the novel so like the writing in his tradition. At the end of the novel the Sheep Man asks, “Heardanythingaboutthewar?” The question goes unanswered, and the novel concludes: “The Benny Goodman Orchestra strikes up ‘Airmail Special.’ Charlie Christian takes a long solo. He is wearing a soft-cream-colored hat.” As Yoshida Kenkô wrote in the fourteenth century: “the pitch of a bell . . . evokes an atmosphere of transience.”

This literary history has skimmed the surface of a profuse literary field. Many minor geniuses, hundreds of skilled literary craftsmen, thousands of dedicated but minor writers, have gone unmentioned. Some of the anointed geniuses of the critical and popular readership have been given short shrift. The riches of the immediate present and the near future barely make an appearance. The history could continue by noting that in recent years many bestselling works of fiction have been cell-phone novels and some of the most serious literary works treating natural and man-made disasters have been on Twitter; or by suggesting that video games are extending the lineage of Japanese literature in their combination of text and image and associative narrative forms, and in their communal reading practice.

The corpus of Japanese literature extends far beyond its national and ethnic boundaries. It encompasses literary writing not just from Japan proper, but from the former Japanese colonies in Taiwan and Korea, from the immigrant communities in Los Angeles, Brazil, Peru, Germany, and Iran. It includes literature written in Japanese by Koreans permanently residing in Japan and also the many volumes of children's stories written in Japanese by the blind Russian Esperantist Vasilii Eroshenko.

The *genius* of Japanese literature lies in its belief that words can access the transcendental by homing in on the concrete and material. Japanese literature has always been open to the direct, sensible literary rendering of this world. It has been both a this-worldly literature, imagining life as dispersed among countless isolated events, and also a literature that lifts its writers and readers off the quotidian plane through glimmers and reverberations—a literature of enchantment. This comes with a caveat: some of the most cherished writers in the tradition are read to this day for the power of their idiosyncratic voices. These are writers whose pronounced goal was to write from life, to assay the personal experience of one's surroundings. They pushed to the limit the tension between the language of realism and the brocade of literary figuration.



From within this thicket of rules and performance practices, which guided the writing of Japanese poetry, there emerged much conventional poetry with no particularly idiosyncratic voice to distinguish it, except perhaps to the fine connoisseur. But in the history of Japanese poetry, there also emerged singular poets who came over the centuries to shine forth on their own. In the imperial anthologies, the most brilliant poets worked within strict conventions to strike a spark of originality, and when they did so the systematic conventionality of the poetry, as if infused by its aesthetic power, seemed to readers, now and then, to reveal the power of real emotion. Here, from the ninth century, is one of Ono no Komachi's most cherished poems, through which she reveals a landscape of inner turmoil. In the following poem, quoted earlier, we glimpse the melancholy mental state that accompanies

**10. A woman bends down to peer into a sake bottle. In this 1854 woodblock print by Utagawa Kuniyoshi, Ono no Komachi, the storied ninth-century master of a poetry of woman's anguish, appears in a picture hanging on a wall, brandishing an umbrella against the whipping rain, as if observing the suffering woman and offering her safety from her storm.**

desuetude in a scene of anguished longing set by moonlight and concluding in ashes:

  no moon lights the night
nor can I meet my lover
  my blazing passion
wakens me my pounding heart
shoots flame then turns into cinders

The poet works from within the strict parameters of allowable form and diction and draws on the deepest resources of Japanese literature: words and rhythms that perform emotion and make one feel emotion's palpable reality; language that refers not to the world itself, but to other language; language that moves beyond itself to places words cannot reach.

# References

## Chapter 1

*Kokinshû: A Collection of Poems Ancient and Modern*, translated by Laurel Rasplica Rodd with Mary Catherine Henkenius (Princeton: Princeton University Press, 1984), 35.

*Shinkokinshû: New Collection of Poems Ancient and Modern* Vol. I, translated and introduced by Laurel Rasplica Rodd (Leiden: Brill, 2015), xxxv.

*Kokinshû: A Collection of Poems Ancient and Modern*, translated by Laurel Rasplica Rodd with Mary Catherine Henkenius (Princeton: Princeton University Press, 1984), 18.

*The Ten Thousand Leaves: A Translation of the Man'yôshû, Japan's Premier Anthology of Classical Poetry Volume One*, translated by Ian Hideo Levy (Princeton: Princeton University Press, 1981), 100–101.

Esperanza Ramirez-Christensen, *Emptiness and Temporality: Buddhism and Medieval Japanese Poetics* (Stanford, CA: Stanford University Press, 2008), 98.

Fujiwara Teika, *Conversations with Shôtetsu Translated by Robert H. Brower; With an Introduction and Notes by Steven D. Carter* (Ann Arbor: University of Michigan Press, 1991), 83.

*Saigyo: Poems of a Mountain Home*, translated by Burton Watson (New York: Columbia University Press, 1992), 22, 8.

Donald Keene, *Nō and Bunraku: Two Forms of Japanese Theatre* (New York,: Columbia University Press, 1991), 23.

*Japanese Nô Dramas*, translated by Royal Tyler (London: Penguin Books, 1992), 213–14.

Kitamura Tôkoku, "Jinsei in aiwataru to wa nan no wake zo," in *Chikuma gendai bungaku taikei* (Tokyo: Chikuma shobô, 1975), 67.
Makoto Ueda, "*Yûgen* and Erhabene: Ônishi Yoshinori's Attempt to Synthesize Japanese and Western Aesthetics," in *Culture and Identity: Japanese Intellectuals During the Interwar Period*, edited by J. Thomas Rimer (Princeton NJ: Princeton University Press, 1990), 294.
*The Essential Haiku: Versions of Bashô, Buson and Issa*, edited with verse translations by Robert Hass (New York: Harper Collins, 1994), 234, 40, 24, 18.
Donald Keene, *The Winter Shines In: A Life of Masaoka Shiki* (New York: Columbia University Press, 2016), 98–9.
*Masaoka Shiki: Selected Poems*, translated by Burton Watson. (New York: Columbia University Press, 2000), 8.
Brendan Morley, *Masaoka Shiki's Letters to the* Tanka *Poets: An annotated translation with introductory essay* (unpublished), 14, 25.
Janine Beichman, *Masaoka Shiki* (Boston: Twayne, 1982), 136, 139.



## Chapter 2

Murasaki Shikibu, *The Tale of Genji*, translated by Dennis Washburn (New York: W. W. Norton, 2015), 200, 152, 305–7, 1319.
Earl Miner, *Comparative Poetics: An Intercultural Essay on Theories of Literature* (Princeton NJ: Princeton University Press, 1990), 45.
Enchi Fumiko, *Masks*, translated by Juliet Winters Carpenter (New York: Knopf, 1983), 56–7.
Nakagami Kenji, *Misaki* (Tokyo: Kawade shobô, 1977), 8.
*The Pillow Book of Sei Shônagon*, translated by Ivan Morris (New York: Columbia University Press, 1991), 30.
*The Tsurezuregusa of Kenkô*, translated by Donald Keene (New York: Columbia University Press, 1967), 7, 170, 139, 192, 182.

## Chapter 3

Mori Ôgai, *Vita Sexualis*, translated by Kazuji Ninomiya and Sanford Goldstein (Rutland, Vermont: Charles Tuttle, 1972), 153.
*The Incident at Sakai and Other Stories*, edited by David Dilworth and J. Thomas Rimer (Honolulu: University of Hawai'i Press, 1977), 116.

Ishikawa Jun, *The Bodhisattva or Samantabhadra*, translated by William Jefferson Tyler (New York: Columbia University Press, 1990), 2.

Nakagami Kenji, *Sennen no yûraku* (Tokyo: Kawade shobô shinsha, 1982), 7.

Shiga Naoya, *A Dark Night's Passing*, translated by Edwin McClellan (Tokyo: Kodansha International, 1993), 401.

Kobayashi Hideo, "Shiga Naoya," in *Chikuma gendai bungaku taikei 43* (Tokyo: Chikuma shobô, 1975), 344.

*Kokinshû: A Collection of Poems Ancient and Modern*, translated by Laurel Rasplica Rodd with Mary Catherine Henkenius (Princeton NJ: Princeton University Press, 1984), 44–6.

Natsume Sôseki, *Theory of Literature and Other Critical Writings*, edited by Michael Bourdaghs, Atsuko Ueda, and Joseph A. Murphy (New York: Columbia University Press, 2009), 28.

Natsume Sôseki, *Kokoro*, translated by Edwin McClellan (Chicago: Regnery Publishing, 1957), 128–9.

Natsume Sôseki, *Theory of Literature and Other Critical Writings*, 52.

Akutagawa Ryûnosuke, "Bungeiteki na anmari ni mo bungeiteki na," in *Nihon kindai bungaku taikei* (Tokyo: Kadokawa shoten, 1970), 8, 26–7, 44, 85.

Tanizaki Jun'ichirô, *In Praise of Shadows*, translated by Edwin G. Seidensticker and Thomas J. Harper (Maine, Sedgwick: Leete's Island Books, 1977), 32–3.

Kawabata Yasunari, *Snow Country*, translated by Edwin G. Seidensticker (Tokyo: Charles Tuttle, 1991), 30–2, 172–5.

Orikuchi Shinobu, *The Book of the Dead, Translated and with an Introduction by Jeffrey Angles* (Minneapolis: University of Minneapolis Press, 2016), 61.



## Chapter 4

*Four Major Plays of Chikamatsu*, translated by Donald Keene (New York: Columbia University Press, 1964), 171–208.

Earl Miner, "The Grounds of Mimetic and Nonmimetic Art: The Western Sister Arts in a Japanese Mirror," in *Articulate Images: The Sister Arts from Hogarth to Tennyson*, ed. Richard Wendorf (Minneapolis: University of Minnesota Press, 1983), 81.

Kamo no Chômei, *An Account of My Hut*, translated by Donald Keene, in Donald Keene, editor, *Anthology of Japanese Literature: Earliest Era to Mid-Nineteenth Century* (New York: Grove Press, 1955), 197.

*The Tales of Heike*, translated by Burton Watson (New York: Columbia University Press, 2008), 9, 70–1.

Yukio Mishima, *Confessions of a Mask*, translated by Meredith Weatherby (New York: New Directions, 1958), 39–40.

Ôe Kenzaburô, *Hiroshima Notes*, translated by David L. Swain and Toshi Yonezawa (New York: Grove, 1981), 104–6.

Ôe Kenzaburô, A *Personal Matter*, translated by John Nathan (New York: Grove, 1994), 71, 84, 89–90, 151.

Ôta Yôko, *City of Corpses*, in *Hiroshima: Three Witnesses*, translated by Richard H. Minear (Princeton NJ: Princeton University Press, 1990), 147, 153, 158–9.

Masuji Ibuse, *Black Rain* (Tokyo: Kodansha International, 1981), 160–1, 300, 127.

*Japanese Death Poems Written by Zen Monks and Haiku Poets on the Verge of Death*, compiled and with an introduction by Yoel Hoffman (Tokyo: Charles Tuttle, 1986), 190, 295.

## Chapter 5

*Taishû bunka jiten*, ed. Ichikawa Hiroshi et al. (Tokyo: Kôbundo, 1991), 796.

Matsuyama Iwao, *Ranpo to Tôkyô: 1920-nen o kao* (Tokyo: Chikuma shobô, 1994), 181–2.

Kôbô Abe, *The Woman in the Dunes*, translated by E. Dale Saunders (Tokyo: Charles Tuttle, 1978), 3.

Nagai Kafû, *A Strange Tale from East of the River*, translated by Edwin G. Seidensticker (Tokyo: Charles Tuttle, 1977), 154–5.

Donald Keene, *The Winter Shines In: A Life of Masaoka Shiki* (New York: Columbia University Press, 2016), 160.

Alan Tansman, *The Writings of Kôda Aya: A Japanese Literary Daughter* (New Haven, CT: Yale University Press, 1993), 127.

"Faasu ni tsuite," in *Sakaguchi Ango* (Tokyo: Chikuma shobô, 1991), 44–5.

Joel Ralph Cohn, *Studies in the Comic Spirit in Modern Japanese Fiction* (Cambridge, MA: Harvard-Yenching Institute, 1998), 143–4.

H. Mack Horton, "Renga Unbound: Performative aspects of Japanese Linked Verse," in *Harvard Journal of Asiatic Studies*, Vol. 53, No. 2 (December, 1993): 449–51, 470.

Tsukioka Settei, *Great Pleasures for Women and Their Treasure Boxes and Love Letters and a River of Erect Precepts for Women*, translated by C. Andrew Gerstle, in *An episodic festschrift for Howard Hibbett* (Hollywood: highmoonnoon, 2009), 13, 15.

## Chapter 6

Makoto Ueda, "*Yûgen* and Erhabene: Ônishi Yohinori's Attempt to Synthesize Japanese and Western Aesthetics," in *Culture and Identity: Japanese Intellectuals during the Interwar Period*, ed. J. Thomas Rimer (Princeton NJ: Princeton University Press, 1990), 294.

*Shinkokinshû: New Collection of Poems Ancient and Modern* Vol. I, translated and introduced by Laurel Rasplica Rodd (Leiden: Brill, 2015), 47.

Paul Roquet, *Ambient Media: Japanese Atmospherics of Self* (Minneapolis: University of Minnesota Press, 2016), 160, 156.

Haruki Murakami, *A Wild Sheep Chase*, translated by Alfred Birnbaum (New York: Penguin Books, 1989), 288.

*Kokinshû: A Collection of Poems Ancient and Modern*, translated by Laurel Rasplica Rodd with Mary Catherine Henkenius (Princeton NJ: Princeton University Press, 1984), 353.

# Further reading

## Translations

Bakin, Kyokutei. *Eight Dogs, or "Hakkenden": Part One—An Ill-Considered Jest*. Translated by Glynne Walley. Ithaca, NY: Cornell University Press: 2021.

Birnbaum, Phyllis. *Rabbits, Crabs, Etc.: Stories by Japanese Women.* Cambridge, MA: Harvard East Asian Monographs, 1984.

Chikamatsu. *Four Major Plays of Chikamatsu.* Translated by Donald Keene. New York: Columbia University Press, 1964.

Dazai Osamu, *The Setting Sun*. Translated by Donald Keene. New York: New Directions Book.

Enchi Fumiko, *Masks*. Translated by Juliet Winters Carpenter. New York: Knopf, 1983.

*The Essential Haiku: Versions of Bashô, Buson and Issa.* Edited with verse translations by Robert Hass. New York: Harper Collins, 1994.

*Hiroshima: Three Witnesses*. Translated by Richard H. Minear. Princeton NJ: Princeton University Press, 1990.

Hirschfeld, Jane and Mariko, Aratani. *The Ink Dark Moon: Love Poems by Ono no Komachi and Izumi Shikibu, Women of the Ancient Court of Japan.* New York: Vintage Books, 1990.

Masuji. *Black Rain*. Translated by John Bester. Tokyo: Kodansha International, 1981.

Ishikawa Jun. *The Bodhisattva or Samantabhadra.* Translated by William Jeffferson Tyler. New York: Columbia University Press, 1990.

*The Izumi Shikibu Diary: A Romance of the Heian Court*. Translated by Edwin Cranston. Cambridge, MA: Harvard University Press, 1969.

*Japanese Death Poems Written by Zen Monks and Haiku Poets on the Verge of Death*. Compiled and with an introduction by Yoel Hoffman. Tokyo: Charles Tuttle, 1986.

*Japanese Nô Dramas* Translated by Royal Tyler. London: Penguin Books, 1992.

Kamo no Chômei. *An Account of My Hut*. Translated by Donald Keene, in Donald Keene, editor, *Anthology of Japanese Literature: Earliest Era to Mid-Nineteenth Century*. New York: Grove Press, 1955.

Kawabata Yasunari, *Snow Country*. Translated by Edwin G. Seidensticker. Tokyo: Charles Tuttle, 1991.

Kôbô Abe, *The Woman in the Dunes*, translated by E. Dale Saunders. Tokyo: Charles Tuttle, 1978.

*Kokinshû: A Collection of Poems Ancient and Modern*. Translated by Laurel Rasplica Rodd with Mary Catherine Henkenius. Princeton NJ: Princeton University Press, 1984.

Lie, John, *Zainichi Literature: Japanese Writings by Ethnic Koreans*. Berkeley: University of California Press, 2008.

Markus, Andrew. *The Willow in Autumn: Ryûtei Tanehiko*. Cambridge, MA: Harvard University Press, 1992.

Mishima, Yukio. *Confessions of a Mask*. Translated by Meredith Weatherby. New York: New Directions, 1958.

Mori Ôgai, *Vita Sexualis*. Ttranslated by Kazuji Ninomiya and Sanford Goldstein. Rutland: Charles Tuttle, 1972.

Mori Ôgai, *The Incident at Sakai and Other Stories*. Edited by David Dilworth and J. Thomas Rimer. Honolulu: University of Hawaii Press, 1977.

Murakami, Haruki. *A Wild Sheep Chase*. Translated by Alfred Birnbaum. New York: Penguin Books, 1989.

Murasaki Shikibu, *The Tale of Genji (Norton critical Editions)*. Translated and edited by Dennis Washburn. New York: W. W. Norton, 2021.

Nagahara Shôson, *Lament in the Night*. Translated by Andrew Leong. Los Angeles: Kaya Press, 2019.

Nakagami Kenji. *The Cape: and Other Stories from the Japanese Ghetto*. Translated by Eve Zimmerman. Berkeley: Stone Bridge, 2008.

Ôe Kenzaburô, *Hiroshima Notes*. Translated by David L. Swain and Toshi Yonezawa. New York: Grove, 1981.

Ôe Kenzaburô, *A Personal Matter*. Translated by John Nathan. New York: Grove, 1994.

*Saigyo: Poems of a Mountain Home*. Translated by Burton Watson. New York: Columbia University Press, 1992.

Saikaku Ihara, *The Great Mirror of Male Love*, translated by Paul Gordon Schalow. Stanford, CA: Stanford University Press, 1990.

Sata Ineko, *Five Faces of Japanese Feminism: Crimson and Other Works*. Translated by Samuel Perry. Honolulu: University of Hawaii Press, 2018.

*The Pillow Book of Sei Shônagon*. Translated by Meredith McKinney. London: Penguin, 2006.

Shiga Naoya, *A Dark Night's Passing*. Translated by Edwin McClellan. Tokyo: Kodansha International, 1993.

*Shinkokinshû: New Collection of Poems Ancient and Modern*, Vol. I. Translated and introduced by Laurel Rasplica Rodd. Leiden: Brill, 2015.

Sôseki, Natsume. *Theory of Literature and Other Critical Writings*. Edited by Michael Bourdaghs, Atsuko Ueda, and Joseph A. Murphy. New York: Columbia University Press, 2009.

Sôseki, Natsume. *Kokoro*. Translated by Edwin McClellan. Chicago: Regnery Publishing, 1957.

*Masaoka Shiki: Selected Poems*. Translated by Burton Watson. New York: Columbia University Press.

*The Tales of Heike*. Translated by Burton Watson. New York: Columbia University Press, 2008.

*Tales of Ise: Lyrical Episodes from Tenth-Century Japan*. Translated by Helen Craig McCullough. Stanford, CA: Stanford University Press, 1968.

Tanizaki Jun'ichirô, *In Praise of Shadows*. Translated by Edwin G. Seidensticker and Thomas J. Harper. Maine: Leete's Island Books, 1977.

Tanizaki Jun'ichirô, *Naomi*. Translated by Anthony H. Chambers. New York: Alfred A. Knopf, 1985.

*The Ten Thousand Leaves: A Translation of the Man'yôshû, Japan's Premier Anthology of Classical Poetry Volume One*. Translated by Ian Hideo Levy. Princeton NJ, Princeton University Press, 1981.

*Three-Dimensional Reading: Stories of Time and Space in Japenese Modernist Fiction*. Edited by Anglea Yiu. Honolulu: University of Hawaii Press, 2013.

*Tokyo Stories: A Literary Stroll*. Translated and edited by Lawrence Rogers. Berkeley: University of California Press, 2002.

*The Tsurezuregusa of Kenkô*. Translated by Donald Keene. New York: Columbia University Press, 1967.

Tsushima Yûko, *Territory of Light*. Translated by Geraldine Harcourt. New York: Farrar, Straus and Giroux, 1979.

Ueda, Makoto. *Bashô and His Interpreters: Selected Hokku*. Stanford, CA: Stanford University Press, 1995.

## Anthologies

*The Columbia Anthology of Modern Japanese Literature*. Vol. 1, *From Restoration to Occupation, 1868–1945*. Edited by J. Thomas Rimer and Van C. and Gessel. New York: Columbia University Press, 2005.

*The Columbia Anthology of Modern Japanese Literature: 1945 to the Present*, Vol. 2. Edited by J. Thomas Rimer and Van C. and Gessel. New York: Columbia University Press, 2005.

*The Columbia Companion to Modern East Asian Literature*. Edited by Joshua S. Mostow, Kirk A. Denton, Bruce Fulton, and Sharalyn Orbaugh. New York: Columbia University Press, 2003.

*An Edo Anthology: Literature from Japan's Mega-City, 1750–1850*. Edited by Sumie Jones, with Kenji Watanabe. Honolulu: University of Hawaii Press, 1994.

Japanese literature resources on the web: https://homepages.wmich.edu/~jangles/jlit.htm

*Modanizumu: Modernist Fiction from Japan, 1913–1938*. Compiled and edited by William J. Tyler. Honolulu: University of Hawaii Press, 2008.

*More Stories by Japanese Women Writers: An Anthology*. Edited by Kyoko Selden and Noriko Mizuta. London: Routledge, 2015.

*The Showa Anthology: Modern Japanese Short Stories 1929–1984*. Edited by Van C. Gessel and Tomone Matsumoto. Kodansha International: 1993.

## Literary studies, biographies, and translations

Danly, Robert Lyons. *In the Shade of Spring Leaves: The Life of Higuchi Ichiyo, with Nine of Her Best Stories*. New York: Norton, 1992.

Doe, Paula. *Warbler's Song in the Dusk: The Life and Work of Otomo Yakamochi*. Berkeley: University of California Press, 1982.

Fraleigh, Matthew. *Plucking Chrysanthemums: Narushima Ryūhoku and Sinitic Literary Traditions in Modern Japan*. Cambridge, MA: Harvard East Asian Monographs, 2016.

Horton, H. Mack. *Song in an Age of Discord: The Journal of Sôchô and Poetic Life in Late Medieval Japan*. Stanford, CA: Stanford University Press, 2002.

Keene, Donald. *The Winter Shines In: A Life of Masaoka Shiki*. New York: Columbia University Press, 2013.

Kern, Adam. *Manga from the Floating World: Comic Book Culture and the Kibyōshi of Edo Japan*. Cambridge, MA: Harvard East Asian Monographs, 2019.

McClellan, Edwin. *Woman in the Crested Kimono: The Life of Shibue Io and Her Family Drawn from Mori Ôgai's Shibue Chûsai*. New Haven, CT: Yale University Press, 1998.

Nathan, John. *Mishima: A Biography*. New York: Da Capo, 1974.

Nathan, John. *Sōseki: Modern Japan's Greatest Novelist*. New York: Columbia University Press, 2018.

Orikuchi Shinobu. *The Book of the Dead*. Translated by Jeffrey Angles. Minneapolis: University of Minnesota Press, 2016.

Seidensticker, Edward. *Kafû the Scribbler: The Life and Writings of Nagai Kafû, 1897*–1959. Ann Arbor: University of Michigan Center for Japanese Studies, 1990.

Tansman, Alan *The Writings of Kôda Aya: A Japanese Literary Daughter*. New Haven, CT: Yale University Press, 1993.



## Scholarly works

Bargen, Doris. *A Woman's Weapon: Spirit Possession in the Tale of Genji*. Honolulu: University of Hawai'i Press, 1997.

Cather, Kirsten. *The Art of Censorship in Postwar Japan*. Hawaii: University of Hawaii Press, 2012.

Chance, Linda H. *Formless in Form: Kenko, Tsurezuregusa, and the Rhetoric of Japanese Fragmentary Prose*. Stanford, CA: Stanford University Press, 1997.

Cohn, Joel Ralph. *Studies in the Comic Spirit in Modern Japanese Fiction*. Cambridge, MA: Harvard-Yenching Institute, 1998.

Ebersole, Gary L *Ritual Poetry and the Politics of Death in Early Japan*. Princeton NJ: Princeton University Press, 1989.

Emmerich, Michael. *The Tale of Genji: Translation, Canonization, and World Literature*. New York: Columbia University Press, 2015.

Golley, Greg. *When Our Eyes No Longer See: Realism, Science, and Ecology in Japanese Literary Modernism*. Cambridge, MA: Harvard East Asian Monographs, 2008.

Hare, Thomas Blenman. *Zeami's Style: The Noh Plays of Zeami Motokiyo*. Stanford, CA: Stanford University Press, 1986.

Harper, Thomas and Shirane Haruo, editors. *Reading The Tale of Genji: Sources from the First Millennium*. New York: Columbia University Press, 2015.

Ito, Ken. *An Age of Melodrama: Family, Gender, and Social Hierarchy in the Turn-of-the-Century Japanese Novel*. Stanford, CA: Stanford University Press, 2008.

Keene, Donald. *The Pleasures of Japanese Literature*. New York: Columbia University Press, 1988.

Levy, Indra. *Sirens of the Western Shore: Westernesque Women and Translation in Modern Japanese Literature*. New York: Columbia University Press, 2010.

Lippit, Seiji M. *Topographies of Japanese Modernism*. New York: Columbia University Press, 2002.

Long, Hoyt. *The Values in Numbers: Reading Japanese Literature in a Global Information Age*. New York: Columbia University Press, 2021.

Lurie, David. *Realms of Literacy: Early Japan and the History of Writing*. Cambridge, MA: Harvard University Asia Center, 2011.

Maeda Ai, *Text and the City: Essays on Japanese Modernity*, edited by James Fujii. Durham, NC: Duke University Press, 2004.

Markus, Andrew, *The Willow in Autumn: Ryûtei Tanehiko*. Cambridge, MA: Harvard University Press, 1992.

Miner, Earl. *Comparative Poetics: An Intercultural Essay on Theories of Literature*. Princeton NJ: Princeton University Press, 1990.

Murasaki Shikibu, *The Tale of Genji (Norton Critical Editions)*. Translated and edited by Dennis Washburn. New York: W. W. Norton, 2021.

Ramirez-Christensen, Esperanza. *Emptiness and Temporality: Buddhism and Medieval Japanese Poetics*. Stanford, CA: Stanford University Press, 2008.

Reichert, James. *In the Company of Men: Representations of Male-Male Sexuality in Meiji Literature*. Stanford, CA: Stanford University Press, 2006.

Roquet, Paul. *Ambient Media: Japanese Atmospherics of Self*. Minneapolis: University of Minnesota Press, 2016.

Sas, Miryam. *Fault Lines: Cultural Memory and Japanese Surrealism*. Stanford, CA: Stanford University Press, 2001.

Schalow, Paul and Walker, Janet. *The Woman's Hand: Gender and Theory in Japanese Women's* Writings. Stanford, CA: Stanford University Press, 1997.

Schmidt-Hori, Sachi. *Tales of Idolized Boys: Male-Male Love in Medieval Japanese Narratives.* University of Hawa'ii Press, 2021.

Shirane, Haruo. *Japan and the Culture of the Four Seasons: Nature, Literature, and the Arts*. New York: Columbia University Press, 2013.

Shirane, Haruo and Suzuki, Tomi, editors. *Inventing the Classics Modernity, National Identity, and Japanese Literature*. Stanford, CA: Stanford University Press, 2002.

Silverberg, Miriam. *Changing Song: The Marxist Manifestos of Nakano Shigeharu.* Princeton NJ: Princeton University Press, 1990.

Torrance, Richard. *The Fiction of Tokuda Shûsei and the Emergence of Japan's New Middle Class*. Seattle: University of Washington Press, 1994.

Treat, John Whittear. *Writing Ground Zero Japanese Literature and the Atomic Bomb*. Chicago: University of Chicago Press, 1995.

Vincent, Keith. *Two-Timing Modernity Homosocial Narrative in Modern Japanese Fiction*. Cambridge, MA: Harvard East Asian Monographs, 2012.

Ueda, Makoto. *Bashô and His Interpreters: Selected Hokku*. Stanford, CA: Stanford University Press, 1995.

Washburn, Dennis. *The Dilemma of the Modern in Japanese Fiction.* New Haven, CT: Yale University Press, 1995.

Yoda, Tomiko. *Gender and National Literature: Heian Texts and the Constructions of Japanese Modernity*. Durham: Duke University Press, 2004.

Zwicker, Jonathan. *Practices of the Sentimental Imagination: Melodrama, the Novel, and the Social Imaginary in Nineteenth-Century Japan*. Cambridge, MA: Harvard University Press, 2006.

# Index

Figures are indicated by an italic *f* following the paragraph number.

## L

## M



## N

## O



## P

## Q



## R

# S



# T

## U



## V



## W

## Z